The True Estimate of Life and How to Live

The True Estimate of Life and How to Live

How to Make Your Life Count for Christ

G. Campbell Morgan

ANEKO PRESS

We enjoy hearing from our readers. Please contact us at www.anekopress.com/questions-comments with any questions, comments, or suggestions.

Cover Designer: Jonathan Lewis
Editors: Jon D. Fogdall and Ruth Clark

Aneko Press
www.anekopress.com
Aneko Press, Life Sentence Publishing, and our logos are trademarks of
Life Sentence Publishing, Inc.
203 E. Birch Street
P.O. Box 652
Abbotsford, WI 54405
RELIGION / Christian Living / Spiritual Growth
Paperback ISBN: 978-1-62245-874-5
eBook ISBN: 978-1-62245-875-2

10 9 8 7 6 5 4 3 2 1

Available where books are sold

Contents

Chapter 1

The Apostle Paul's Estimate of Life

In the history of the Christian church, it is likely that the world has never seen anyone so wondrously live out the character and conduct of Christianity as the apostle Paul did. Most of us will agree that he understood more fully than any one of his contemporaries the purposes of God as revealed in Jesus Christ. Paul's life and teaching have revealed the meaning of Christianity in a way that nobody else has. It is very interesting in his letter to the Philippians, one of his later epistles, to find him writing about himself, principally in the new life, which at that time he had been living for about thirty-three years. He writes with human tenderness, of human sensibilities, and with human thoughts, while yet upon all of these there rests the light of the Divine, and through it all there is manifested the power that has taken possession of him.

In this epistle, written to his children in the faith at Philippi, it is evident that he writes under the stress of circumstances. Those circumstances are not causing him one moment of anxiety, but they do compel him to face the alternative possibilities before him. This is the condition in which he writes this letter and condenses into one swift, burning sentence an epitome of Christianity as he knows it: *For to me, to live is Christ* (Philippians 1:21).

To Paul, all of the marvelous revelations of the doctrine and the scheme of redemption can be condensed and expressed in these simple words. He tells the whole story of his own experience of Christianity when he writes, *For to me, to live is Christ.* To him, Christianity is Christ.

> Christ! I am Christ! and let the name suffice you,
> Ay, for me too He greatly hath sufficed;
> Christ is the end, for Christ was the beginning,
> Christ the beginning, for the end is Christ.

These statements in F. W. H. Myers' poem "Saint Paul" of the apostle's view of Christianity gather force when we remember the circumstances under which he wrote it. Paul was a prisoner guarded by the Praetorian Guard. He was waiting, most likely, for the final word of the emperor which would decide which of two paths he would walk. If the emperor commands death, the apostle will walk through his prison door and through the city to the place of his execution. Then by one swift, sudden stroke his life will end. He looks at that path and thinks about walking it. Then he looks in the other direction.

Suppose that the emperor commands that he be set free. Then he will hurry back to Philippi to see his spiritual children. Then he will hurry off to some new region to tell the same story, live the same life, and win more trophies for Christ. He looks at these two paths stretching before him, and he says, *For to me, to live is Christ and to die is gain. But I am hard-pressed from both directions, having the desire to depart and be with Christ, for that is very much better; yet to remain on in the flesh is more necessary for your sake* (Philippians 1:21, 23-24).

Life and death have lost their old significance to him because there is one vision that fills the horizon no matter which way he looks. Here it is Christ, and there it is gain, and gain is Christ, and Christ is gain. There is no darkness but only light, for everywhere he sees the Master. That is Christianity.

I want to meditate on that understanding of Christian life. I cannot cover all of the possibilities, for in this text lie all of the possibilities and potentialities of the Christian life.

For to me, to live is Christ. What did the apostle mean? There are seven things which he may have meant:

1. Christ was the author of his life. It was as though he had written, "To me to live at all is Christ."

2. Christ was the sustainer of his life. "To me to continue to live is Christ."

3. Christ was the law of his life. "The conditions in which I live my life are summed up in Christ."

4. Christ was the product of his life. "To me to live is to reproduce Christ."

5. Christ was the aim and influence of his life. "To me to live is to lead men to Christ."

6. Christ was the impulse of his life. "To me to live is to be swept along under the compassion of Christ."

7. Christ was the finisher, the crown of his life. "To me to live is at last to be what He is, and to find the crowning of all my manhood in Him."

Christ is the end, as Christ was the beginning. Christ is the beginning, and therefore Christ is the end. Whether Paul looked back upon the past, at the present, or into the future, within or without, behind, above, or beyond to the consummation – wherever he looked, he saw only Jesus.

The first thought is that when Paul wrote these words: *For to me, to live is Christ,* he meant to say, "Christ is the author of my life."

Paul did not think that he had any life except the life which was named "Christ." His life began the day when Christ was born in him through the power of the Holy Spirit. In the life of Paul, there is one clean line dividing his life. Behind that line is the old life, the "old man," to which he so often referred. On the other side of the line is the new life, the "new man." To Paul, the crossing of that line went to the very depths of his being. It transformed him so much that in looking back to the days before he became a new man in Christ, he said of the old days, *The old things passed away* (2 Corinthians 5:17). They had vanished out of his sight. He did not regard as important anything that was behind him. He said, *New things have come,* and he lived in the new things. The years that he spent on the earth prior to the moment when Jesus found him, he did not consider worth talking about for a single moment.

Wasn't Paul mistaken? Hadn't he accomplished a lot in the years before his conversion? Stop him for a moment and ask him, "Paul, what do you mean? You lived a very remarkable life before you met Jesus of Nazareth. You were taught at the feet of Gamaliel. You had all the advantages of learning and religion. You had never been recklessly extravagant. Your life had been straight and pure, clean through. You were a Pharisee of the Pharisees, a Hebrew of the Hebrews. Outwardly, and infinitely more importantly, in all inward sincerity, you were a remarkable man."

"Perfectly true; *but whatever things were gain to me, those things I have counted as loss for the sake of Christ*" (Philippians 3:7).

"Why?"

"Because I compared what I found when Christ found me.

4

When I turned my back upon the old, I did it forever, because my face was set toward the new."

I do not think Paul gave even five minutes of his time wondering if he should go back to his old life once a week for his enjoyment, and then live the new life for the rest of the week as a matter of duty. His old life *passed away,* and his new life opened before him bright with joy, thrilling delights, and getting better all the way.

Paul's new life began when a light shined on him on the way to Damascus. We learn so much by contrast. Look at him for a moment on the way to Damascus. Remember that he was straight, upright, moral, righteous, sincere to the core of his being. He carried in his hand some very important documents – letters from the high priest. What for? Because in Damascus there was a small group of men and women who were daring to turn from the empty religion of their fathers. They were now singing hymns about this Jesus, whom Paul's friends had crucified. If they were to continue singing their hymns, they would soon undermine the national religion. Paul was going to put an end to it. While he was riding to Damascus with the priest's letters in his possession, a light fell from heaven, and a voice from heaven spoke. Paul fell to the ground and said to the voice from heaven, *"Who are You, Lord?"*

The revelation that came to him must have been the most startling in his life: *"I am Jesus whom you are persecuting."*

Always remember what Paul said here: *"Lord."*

What a change! Paul has joined the church at Damascus even before he arrives there! That is all they are doing, calling Jesus *Lord,* and Paul has done it. See the radical nature of this change? Do you see that he has taken the crown of his life from off his own head and has put it on the head of Jesus?

And what else? *Lord, what wilt thou have me to do?* (Acts 9:6 KJV).

That is, from that point on, the keynote of his life. The music is true to it through the rest of his life. Through missionary journeys, through perils by land and by sea, in prison and among robbers, when suffering persecutions, or preaching the gospel of the grace of God, he is always true to the question he asked: *Lord, what wilt thou have me to do?* His life began there. His old life dropped away, and the new life opened before him. Looking back to that beginning from the jail in Rome, he wrote, *For to me, to live is Christ.*

Life began there. We can judge how real the change was by asking him a question, which I often think I will ask him when I meet him in heaven: "Paul, haven't you forgotten the ride to Damascus?"

"No, I still remember the hour my Lord apprehended me."

"But Paul, what did you do with the high priest's letters?"

Did you ever think of that? I want to know. They were removed from his life like everything else of his old life. *Old things passed away.*

That was Paul's spiritual birthday. When is your spiritual birthday? Let me say something for the sake of those who say, "I do not have a spiritual birthday." A question like that may cause your soul to tremble and become unsettled. The devil will readily take hold of anything that he can use to unsettle you. If your doubt says to you, "You don't have a spiritual birthday," say, "If I never had one, I will have one now." If a definite is needed, claim today and say to God right now the words W. McDonald wrote in the hymn, *I Am Coming to the Cross:*

> Here I give my all to thee,
>> Friends and time, and earthly store;
> Soul and body Thine to be,
>> Wholly Thine forevermore.

The Master says, *"The one who comes to Me I will certainly not cast out"* (John 6:37). We have the date, and any "now" will do. So we will dismiss the devil and move on. The point is that there is a passing into the new life and a turning of the back upon the old life. *For to me, to live is Christ.* Bless the fact of regeneration, to which we owe everything that comes after it! All of the new possibilities which God offers to us are the result of the fact that the Master stopped us and gave us His life, so that our old things passed away and all things became new.

But Paul means infinitely more. He also means, "To me to continue to live is Christ." For about thirty-three years he has been following Jesus. The music of his life has been playing amid earth's lamentations. The harmonies have been varied, but that has always been the chord of the dominant.

But what does he mean when he says that to him, "to continue to live is Christ"?

It is Paul's confession of his own helplessness. He says, "Here I am after thirty-three years, by the grace of God. I am still living the same life that began then."

"But how?"

"By Christ. I have not kept Him, He has kept me. I have not clung to the cross; the Man of the cross has clung to me, which is infinitely better. He has sustained my life during these thirty-three years."

Beloved in Christ, do we sufficiently grasp that great truth for ourselves? Weak, trembling men and women, who have started the Christian life, are crying and wondering how they will hold out. If it is left to you, you will leave the path. If it is left to me, I will soon be a castaway.

You remember that wonderful figure of speech from the lips of Jesus recorded in the Gospel of John? Christ says that He is not only the author but also the sustainer of life. *"I am the vine, you are the branches"* (John 15:5). Put it into other words to bring out the inner thought. People have an idea that Jesus meant to say, "I am the main stem of the vine, and you are the branches grafted into Me. Through Me, the main stem, all the forces of life pass into you the branches."

That is very beautiful, but Jesus meant something infinitely stronger.

What did he say? *I am* – not the main stem – *I am the vine.* What is the vine? Root, main stem, branches, leaves, tendrils, fruit – everything. That is the vine. People speak as though the main stem alone was the vine, held up by roots and expressing itself in branches. That is true in a sense, but I take this word of Christ's in its simplicity, and therefore in its sublimity. *I am the vine* – all of it. What does this mean? *You are the branches* – part of the vine – and the life of the branch is the life of the vine.

In a sense the vine gives its life to the branch, but not as a separate thing. The branch is part of the vine, and the very life that courses through the branch and reproduces itself in fruit is the life of the vine. *For to me, to live is Christ.* Christ's life sustains me. It is He Himself in me. I am His; He is mine. We are one by a solemn union, a union infinitely beyond anything that metaphors or figures of speech can teach, one with each other, and by that fact of our oneness my life has been sustained. *For to me, to live is Christ.*

I love this third thought when he said, *For to me, to live is Christ* – Christ is the condition of my life; Christ is the law of my life.

That is why Paul was angry with the Galatians. He said to them, *You foolish Galatians. You were running well; who hindered you?* (Galatians 3:1; 5:7).

Why did he say they had been hindered? They were going back to the outward sign of circumcision, rather than the circumcision of the heart by faith. Paul said, *How is it that you turn back again to the weak and worthless elemental things, to which you desire to be enslaved all over again?* (Galatians 4:9).

How is it with you, Paul?

"*For to me, to live is Christ;* not a set of man-made, unbiblical rules, but a life principle within me. Not living my life by timetables, sayings, and rules, but by allowing the ever-present Christ to stretch me to the limits of my being, and by allowing His presence to direct my whole life within the bounds of His own sacred will."

Paul lived in the new covenant that Jeremiah spoke about, the covenant in which the law is no longer written on stone tablets, but on his heart. If a person wanted to know what God wanted him to do, he would not need to go to a temple, a priest, an altar, or a code of rules. He would only need to turn to God in the silence and quietness of his heart, and say,

> O strong life of God in Christ who lives in me,
> Direct, control, guide me today
> In all I think, do, or say,
> That all my efforts with all their might,
> May for thy glory only unite.

Paul lived there. He had a fresh code of ethics every morning, a new list of regulations every moment; and these all came from the impulse of the Christ-life within him. Christ was the law of his life; Christ conditioned his days; and Christ was the author, the sustainer, and the law.

It is as though Paul had said, "Christ is the product of my life. *For to me, to live is Christ.*"

But if anyone says that, and there is no manifestation of it in their life, who will believe him? Not I. I am quite sure that Paul did not want anyone to believe him unless it was perfectly evident in his life.

Suppose that someone is living a life that is selfish, malicious, proud, critical, and unkind, and he says, "*For to me, to live is Christ.*"

Do not blaspheme! Your life is selfish, your life is malicious, your life is critical, your life is unkind; was Jesus any of these things?

"Oh no," he says, "I do not mean that. I mean that I have accepted His principles."

Never! No one ever really accepted the principles who did not get Christ first. The principles grow out of the living Christ; and when that is so, the principles are forever manifesting themselves in that person.

Do you not see the necessity for this? Nature, so far as we understand it, always reproduces itself true to type. I remember when I planted flowers in my garden in Birmingham. I went down to a shop and bought some bulbs, because I wanted a fine show of tulips in the earlier days of the year. I carefully planted all of them in my garden. I even arranged them according to a color and geometric scheme. I could almost imagine what they would look like. I love God's flowers, though I do not understand them. Winter passed; spring came, and the bulbs came up, but they were crocuses. Why? Because I had planted crocus bulbs. I thought I had bought a bargain and the result was: what I had sowed, I reaped.

Now understand that great principle of life and apply it to this question of sainthood. If the life planted in you is the life of Christ, that then must reproduce itself true to type. If a man always sings, "I want to be an angel," he will be greatly disappointed because he does not have anything that remotely looks like wings anywhere on him. But if a man sings reverently, with deep emotion and earnest desire, "I want to be like Jesus," that is possible. Why? Because the life he lives, if he is born again, is the Christ-life, and if the life of Christ is planted in him, it will on its own reproduce itself, and he will, individually as well as with the church, grow up into Him in all things who is the Head, even Christ.

Let us try to understand this better by looking at two illustrations from Paul's life.

We just saw him on the way to Damascus. I have the deepest admiration for Saul of Tarsus before he was converted. I love a man who is sincere and all-out in anything. But do you see what Paul's sincerity did for him in those old days? It made him say, in effect, "I am sincere and I am determined that the religion of my God shall be *the* religion. If men will not bow to it, then I will put them in prison, and to death. My sincerity arouses my indignation. I am determined to kill men who will not live by that which is a divinely revealed religion."

There he is, a magnificent man, the best that human nature can ever do for a man apart from Jesus Christ. Do not forget it.

There is no better example of the fallen human nature than Saul of Tarsus before Christ found him.

Thirty years later we see Paul before Agrippa and his friends, who desire to amuse themselves by looking at this strange man and hearing what he has to say. Paul gives his testimony and tells the story of how Jesus found and transformed him. Agrippa, looking at him, did not say, "You almost persuade me," but with scorn Agrippa said, *"In a short time you will persuade me to become a Christian"* (Acts 26:28).

What does Paul say? Is he any less sincere and consecrated than he was when he rode to Damascus? No. Is he less enthusiastic? No. Is there any difference? Yes, a huge difference! How does he show it? Handcuffs are on his wrists and chains are on his ankles, but he looks into the face of Agrippa and says, *"I would wish to God, that whether in a short or long time, not only you, but also all who hear me this day, might become such as I am, except for these chains"* (Acts 26:29). He is saying, "I do not want you to wear my chains, Agrippa. Take my Christ, take my light, take my life, but I would not put these chains on even you, Agrippa."

Do you see any change in Paul? Perfectly sincere thirty years earlier, but if you did not agree with him, he would put you to death. Perfectly sincere now, but with an entirely changed tone: "O King Agrippa, if we could only change places and you not wear my chains, I would not harm or distress you for a minute!"

If someone lives Christ, he reproduces Christ. Is that not what Paul did? Are not his words the living echo of that wonderful prayer: *"Father, forgive them; for they do not know what they are doing"* (Luke 23:34)? People always reproduce Christ in some degree when they live His life. If the Christ-life is present in your life, it must come out through the glory on your face, the tenderness of your touch, and a new love for everybody. The very best testimony that you can ever give to the power of Jesus Christ is to live His life – not by your own effort, but by the propulsion of that same life within you. "For me to live is to reproduce Christ."

Let me mention the other points briefly. "To me to live is to influence men toward Christ. The *aim* of my life is Christ."

Do you think that very many of the soldiers who were guarding Paul left without being influenced for Christ? I do not. Every soul that Paul came in contact with was an opportunity. Paul's whole life, so far as active service went, was poured out doing this one thing: bringing men who had never seen Christ to the place where they might see Him, and building up those who had seen Him in their most holy faith from height to height, and from glory unto glory. The whole aim and influence of his life was Christ.

Again, the *impulse* of his life was Christ.

I use the word *impulse* in reference to the great force behind it which propelled him to serve. Consider this illustration. You know the epistle to the Romans, or rather, you know where it is in the Bible. Well, read it again. I propose that you do not understand it yet. I am just beginning to see light upon it, beautiful gleams of glory on it.

Romans chapter 5 speaks of justification; chapter 6, the question of sin; chapter 7, the question of sin still discussed; chapter 8, no condemnation, the larger, purer life; chapter 9, what is in that chapter? Do not read chapter 9 without reading the last verses of chapter 8. What is the highest height of experience in chapter 8? *For I am convinced that neither death, nor life, nor angels, nor principalities, nor things present, nor things to come, nor powers, nor height, nor depth, nor any other created thing, will be able to separate us from the love of God, which is in Christ Jesus our Lord* (Romans 8:38-39).

I always think of Paul here as on a high mountain peak looking at his enemies. They are all around him: death, life, angels, principalities, powers, and things present; and then his imagination sweeps him into all the infinite possibilities of the future: things to come, height, depth, and any other creation. Those are all the possibilities of danger. He declares, "I am convinced that nothing will be able to separate me from the love of God, which is in Christ Jesus my Lord." There he is at the height of vision, the height of experience.

What next? *I am telling the truth in Christ, I am not lying, my conscience testifies with me in the Holy Spirit, that I have great sorrow and unceasing grief in my heart* (Romans 9:1-2).

Romans 8:38-39 does not sound like that! Those verses are a shout of triumph: Nothing can separate Paul from His love! But Paul has great sorrow and constant grief in his heart.

What is Paul grieving about? About himself? No; his self died in the struggle of the preceding chapters. What is he grieving about? *For I could wish that I myself were accursed, separated from Christ for the sake of my brethren, my kinsmen according to the flesh* (Romans 9:3). What is that? It is, *For to me, to live is Christ.* Paul states that the impulse of his life is the Christ-impulse. The passion that brought Christ down to redeem men consumed Paul, and when he touched the highest height of his life, he knew that nothing could separate him from the love of Christ. Then Paul learned the deepest experience of all – that of fellowship in His suffering. For that experience he wished he could be accursed. Jesus Himself was made a curse for us, and Paul was living the Christ-life. For that reason he could say,

> Oft when the Word is on me to deliver
> Lifts the illusion and the truth lies bare;
> Desert or throng, the city or the river,
> Melts in a lucid paradise of air, –
>
> Only like souls I see the folk thereunder,
> Bound who should conquer, slaves who should be kings, –
> Hearing their one hope with an empty wonder,
> Sadly contented in a show of things; –
>
> Then with a rush the intolerable craving
> Shivers throughout me like a trumpet-call, –
> Oh, to save these, to perish for their saving,
> Die for their life, be offered for them all!
> — F. W. H. Myers

Commentators must stop their foolish attempts to explain away those verses. Paul was nearer to Jesus Christ at this point than ever before. This impulse of the Christ-life which brought redemption to man at the cost of Christ's own life enters a human soul and floods it to overflowing, until Paul says, *For I could wish that I myself were accursed, separated from Christ for the sake of my brethren, my kinsmen according to the flesh* (Romans 9:3).

What is the last thing? *Christ is the crown.* He is not only the author, He is also the finisher. He not only began, He will also end the good work.

And when it ends, what is it? Christ. What is the music of the land to come? Christ. What is the fellowship? Christ, and Christ reproduced in the saints. What will be my chief joy when I look again in the face of my child who has died and is waiting for me in heaven? It will be that she is like Jesus. Not only will we see Christ Himself, but also Christ reproduced in our loved ones.

Imagination is sometimes ahead of truth. Poetry guesses at more than prose ever fathoms. Follow the thought, and everywhere, on the throne, and amid the multitudes, what do you see? Christ. That is why Paul stood and, in spite of Nero's threatened axe, said, *To die is gain.*

"Don't you see the executioner, Paul?"

"No, I do not see him."

"What do you see?"

"Christ! *To die is gain.*"

Finish this theme for yourself. Imagine that you have a clean piece of paper in your hand. Write about yourself. God help you! Take a pencil and write! Write the story of your life, honestly, faithfully, truly, in a brief sentence like Paul wrote his story.

Write, "To me to live is money." If that is true, write it.

In God's name, be honest. If you have ever been a hypocrite, do not be one now. Write it down, not for man's eyes, but for God's. Write, "To me to live is money."

"To me to live is pleasure."

"To me to live is fame."

"To me to live is _____."

Fill it in for yourself!

You have now written your life's story. You may never have looked it squarely in the face like this before. There it is, right in front of you, the self-evident truth, the inner meaning of your whole life.

Now finish it. Write what Paul wrote under what you wrote, your statement of life. Write Paul's statement of death: "To me to live is money; to die is – I cannot write *gain* after that. To die is *loss*. When I die, I will leave everything behind me. *'Naked I came from my mother's womb, and naked I shall return there'*" (Job 1:21).

"To me to live is pleasure; to die – oh! do not talk to me about death! It is the last thing I want to think about. I want my pleasure, my laughter, *for as the crackling of thorn bushes under a pot, so is the laughter of the fool; and this too is futility* (Ecclesiastes 7:6); it is all I have! Let me have it, but in God's name do not talk about death. Why do I not like to walk down the street in the dark? Because I think of death. I cannot write that.

"To me to live is fame; to die – no, I cannot. If my name is inscribed on a marble monument, as soon as it is erected, nature will begin to destroy it with mossy fingers. I cannot write, 'To die is to perish, to be forgotten'! What is fame when I am dead? I cannot write it."

No, you cannot write Paul's estimate of death after anything except after Paul's estimate of life. If, by God's great grace you can write, *For to me, to live is Christ,* then you can also write, *To die is gain.* To die is to see Him more clearly, to be closer to Him, to enter into larger service for Him, to touch the height and the depth and the length and the breadth of His life. *To die is gain.* You can only write it if you write, *For to me, to live is Christ.*

Somebody else says, "I have never written, *For to me, to live is Christ.* Can I start?"

Yes.

"Where can I start?"

Where Paul started.

"Where did Paul start?"

Paul said, *Lord, what wilt thou have me to do?*

That is where you start. Will you say that?

"Yes, I will say it and do it. Is it easy?"

No, it is not easy. The cross is there; crucifixion is there; the ending of self is there; the abandoning of everything – of hope, and wife, and child, and home, and friends, and ambition – all is there. Say, "Lord, I have had other lords. Lord, I have been living for myself. I have been governed by human desires. I have been mastered by passions. I have been swept along by my own ambitions. Lord, remove these other lords and You be my King."

That is the place to begin. There is not a man or woman who begins there honestly to whom He will not come with healing on His wings, and the sun rising. Then your old things will pass away and all things will become new.

Chapter 2

Health of Spirit

*H*oliness is simply another word for *health*. Both words are derived from the old Anglo-Saxon word *halig,* which means "whole and complete." It is perfectly correct to speak of a holy body and a healthy spirit, but we have come to speak of bodily holiness as health, and of spiritual health as holiness. Holiness is not maturity, it is not finality; it is rather a condition for growth into maturity and unto finality.

Philippians 3 gives a brief autobiographical sketch of the apostle Paul. He first makes mention of the old life in which he formerly had confidence, and in which he would still have confidence if he were to continue to measure things by the standards of the flesh. Then he goes on to declare that the things that had been gain to him, he now counted as loss for Christ. Notice what he says: *But whatever things were gain to me, those things I have counted as loss for the sake of Christ. More than that, I count all things to be loss in view of the surpassing value of knowing Christ Jesus my Lord* (Philippians 3:7-8a).

In the past, on the way to Damascus, he *counted as loss* the things in which he had prided himself. In the moment when he surrendered himself, absolutely, with all his hopes, and aspirations, and prejudices – everything – to Christ, he said, *Lord, what wilt thou have me to do?* Over thirty years later he writes that he still *count[s] all things to be loss.* He has not abandoned the position he took up so long ago. It is because he is in this same position that he is still in the place of blessing and power. Yet he is not satisfied.

What else is Paul seeking? To answer this question we need to look at these two statements. First, *Not that I have already obtained it or have already become perfect, but I press on so that I may lay hold of that for which also I was laid hold of by Christ Jesus* (Philippians 3:12). Then, *Let us therefore, as many as are perfect, have this attitude; and if in anything you have a different attitude, God will reveal that also to you* (Philippians 3:15). In these two statements the word *perfect* is used to suggest a contradiction. In the first verse, Paul declares that he is not perfect. In the second verse, Paul claims to be perfect. These words in the original manuscript that were translated as *perfect* are not the same. The first verse could read: "Not that I have already obtained it or have already become perfected." The second verse reads: *Let us therefore, as many as are perfect.*

The difference between being perfected and being perfect is the difference between maturity of Christian life and holiness; it is the difference between the condition that is a present possibility, and the condition which cannot be attained until the Lord comes and changes our body of humiliation, and conforms it to the body of His glory. I will be perfected when I see Him as He is; my whole nature, even this body, will be transformed into perfect likeness to Himself. I cannot be perfected here, but I can be perfect in the sense of whole, healthy, and holy.

Paul uses the figure of a race to illustrate the Christian life, and what he says I think may be paraphrased in this way: "I am not perfected yet, I am not crowned yet; the Lord captured me not because of this place of temptation and conflict, but because of the brightness of the joyful day when He will present me – whom He found so depraved – in the very presence of God faultless as He Himself is faultless.

That is the goal of my running, and the crowning point which I have not yet reached; but let us, therefore, as many as be perfect – as many of us as are running the race – continue in the strength and energy of the Holy Spirit, with every weight and sin laid aside, and with the very joy and love of God possessing us." This is how we can be perfect. It is the difference between the crown upon the brow, and the passionate attitude of life which has the crown in view, forgetting all that is behind, pressing toward it with full and complete purpose of life.

That condition of life is the condition of health of spirit before God; it is the condition of perfection in the present moment; and it is a condition which should mark every child of God from the moment of conversion.

The blossom on the tree is perfect, beautifully perfect, but it is not perfected. It is not consummated, it is not mature. It needs the ministry of sun, and rain, and atmosphere to ripen it into perfection. Not until the fires of autumn have acted on it, and it stands in all the glory of perfect fruit will it be perfected.

Put a 6-month-old child next to a 40-year-old man; what a difference! They are both perfect, but the man is perfected with the perfection of maturity, while the child is not.

To reach this perfection of health we must first remember that holiness is the work of God in the life of the believer. To emphasize this, look at four passages of Scripture.

Philippians 2:12-13: *So then, my beloved, . . . work out your salvation with fear and trembling; for it is God who is at work in you, both to will and to work for His good pleasure.*

It is God. I am to work out what God works in. I cannot work out more than God works in. It is only when we see this that we come into the place of health and blessing.

First Thessalonians 5:23-24: *Now may the God of peace Himself sanctify you entirely; and may your spirit and soul and body be preserved complete, without blame at the coming of our Lord Jesus Christ. Faithful is He who calls you, and He also will bring it to pass.* Paul writes, *He also will bring it to pass.* We are not the ones who must preserve blameless these three great elements of our being; it is God who alone is able to do this. All we have to do is lean on Him and understand that it is His work.

Hebrews 13:20-21: *Now the God of peace, who brought up from the dead the great Shepherd of the sheep through the blood of the eternal covenant, even Jesus our Lord, equip you in every good thing to do His will, working in us that which is pleasing in His sight, through Jesus Christ, to whom be the glory forever and ever. Amen.* Notice that the power that sanctifies is the power that brought the Lord Jesus back to life after He died. The one humanly impossible thing in all the ages was the resurrection of a man from the dead, but the fabric of Christianity rests upon the accomplishment of that very thing. The stupendous power that brought Him up from the dead is the power that brings about my sanctification and my perfection. It is dependent not upon my poor feeble attempts, but upon the power of God who brought our Lord Jesus Christ back to life.

Jude 1:24-25: *Now to Him who is able to keep you from stumbling, and to make you stand in the presence of His glory blameless with great joy, to the only God our Savior, through Jesus Christ our Lord, be glory, majesty, dominion and authority, before all time and now and forever. Amen.* The true rendering of *keep you from stumbling* is not just to keep or protect us from falling; what else is it? It is also *to make you stand in the presence of His glory blameless;* not only blameless, but also faultless. There is the perfect and the perfected. We are able to be perfect because He is able to keep us from stumbling; we may be perfected because He is able to present us faultless before the presence of His glory.

The forgiveness of my sins at the cross depends upon Him; the power that heals and keeps me whole depends upon Him; my sanctification hour by hour depends upon Him; and my final presentation before the presence of His glory depends upon Him. The proportion that we see that He is able to do this is the proportion that we will come into the place of blessing.

But while it is His *work,* the responsibility rests on me, that I am in the place where God can do that work, that I have the attitude to which He will respond with His power.

That attitude is declared in 2 Corinthians 6:17-18: *"Therefore, come out from their midst and be separate," says the Lord. "And do not touch what is unclean; and I will welcome you. And I will be a father to you, and you shall be sons and daughters to Me," says the Lord Almighty.*

That is the attitude of separation and renunciation. God does not call us to renounce the great underlying principle of sin; we cannot do that. God cleanses us from that. But He does call us to renounce sin as something which we commit of our own free will.

There are three phases of that sin.

First, *sin is lawlessness.* This definition of sin is perhaps the most profound of all. It includes both the underlying principle and the outwardly expressed activity. I am using it now, however, only in the sense of willful action. *Everyone who practices sin also practices lawlessness; and sin is lawlessness* (1 John 3:4). Everyone believes that. It is the simple, everyday definition of sin. In other words, sin is doing wrong.

Second, *to one who knows the right thing to do and does not do it, to him it is sin* (James 4:17). Sin is neglecting to do what is right.

Many people agree that the first definition is correct, but they

23

do not agree with the second definition. Many are prepared to admit that sin is wrongdoing, but they have not learned that the omission of anything, no matter how simple, when we profess to be a Christian, is sin.

Third, *whatever is not from faith is sin* (Romans 14:23). This definition goes even deeper. If I wonder, as a Christian, whether some action is right or wrong, and I continue to do it while still being doubtful about it, I am sinning because my action is *not from faith*.

Scores of young believers, if they could only see and believe that, would be saved from asking many questions. They ask, "Is it right for me to go here or there, to do this or that?"

The fact that the question arises proves that, at least for the present, it is wrong. The moment you are doubtful about a certain course of action, your solemn duty is to stop that action. In the doing of that doubtful action, that is actual sin against God. There may be something which has been perfectly legitimate for you, but suddenly, in your own communion, in the midst of doing a service for God, that thing appears in a new light and causes you to say, "I wonder if that is right."

The moment the doubt is suggested, the only course open is to stop doing that thing. In the process of time you may be able to go back to it because the doubt may be removed, but you cannot afford to let anything about which there is a suspicion of doubt stand between you and your personal communion with God. The moment you begin to do it you are in the arena of sin.

We are called upon today, so far as our will is concerned, to say, "Lord, we will put away actual wrongdoing out of our lives. We will come into the place of quick and ready obedience; to Your will, when You will make it known anywhere – in our houses, in our habits, in our inward life – there will be no resistance. We will stop doing anything about which we have doubt."

Again, there is not only to be separation and renunciation, but there is also to be the surrender of my whole being to God. *Therefore I urge you, brethren, by the mercies of God, to present your bodies a living and holy sacrifice, acceptable to God, which is your spiritual service of worship* (Romans 12:1).

No one word seems to convey all that is meant by *surrender. Consecration* is a blessed word, but people seem to think that consecration means coming every now and then to give ourselves up to God again. We cannot reconsecrate and reconsecrate, though we may repeatedly recall the perpetual fact of our consecration. The word that helps me more than any other in marking my attitude toward God is the word *abandonment*. It is a mighty word filled with weakness. It indicates my falling back upon God.

"But what about consequences?"

I have nothing to do with consequences.

"But God may completely take me out of the place where I am."

I have nothing to do with that. Whether it is in China, India, America, England, or heaven, I do not care. That is surrender; that is abandonment, if I know anything about it. "Lord, do what You want with me, in all the relations of my life, in all the avenues of my being, everywhere and always." *Present your bodies a living and holy sacrifice, acceptable to God, which is your spiritual service of worship* (Romans 12:1).

Now by God's grace renounce sin, cut a clear line of separation between the old life and the new, so far as actual wrong is concerned, so far as the will is concerned. You cannot give up your wrongdoing unless you get the energy of God. You cannot get the energy of God until you are willing to give up your wrongdoing. So long as you cling to sin, or neglect what you should do, or do doubtful things, you will not get God's blessing. Let the sin go and cast yourself upon God.

And then what?

Believe. Abandon and believe. I do not know which comes first. They go together.

Some may say, "We will abandon, but we cannot trust."

Then you do not abandon. There is no value in standing on the edge of a sheet of ice and saying that it will bear my weight, while you will not go on it. Get out on it, man! Believe and abandon yourself to Him in one great act. Oh friend, longing as you are for holiness, will you quit your sin and fall back upon God?

You cannot live the blessed life by your own effort, but you can if *He* lives it in you by His own overwhelming grace. He has taught me that *I* cannot, but *He* can.

Little things keep men and women from this blessed life! In 1895 I went to Douglas, on the Isle of Man, and in one of my afternoon meetings a young lady came to me and said that all the joy had gone out of her life four years ago.

"Praise God," I said.

"What about?" she asked.

"That you know when it went; because if you know when it went, you know how it went."

She said, "I don't think I do."

"Yes, you do; you are very definite about the time. Go back four years and tell me what happened."

She hung her head for a while, and I knew that something had happened.

"What was it?" I asked.

She replied, "I disagreed with my oldest friend. We were both Christians, and I wanted to tell her that I was wrong, but I didn't. She has left the country."

"Well," I said, "it is evident that you know the reason for your failure."

"What should I do?" she asked.

"Write to her and tell her that you were wrong; that is what the Master wanted you to do then."

"I can't do that."

"You will never get your joy back until you do."

She came to all of the meetings and fought God. She had all the knowledge of the blessed life that had come to her from her past experiences, yet she was in darkness because she would not go back to the point of disobedience and be obedient.

The next year I returned to Douglas. My first meeting was for workers. One of the first people I spoke to was that young woman. The first thing I said to her was, "Did you send that letter?"

She said, "Yes," and every line on her face convinced me that her joy had returned. She said, "I wrote it last night! I have been fighting God for twelve months about that letter. All last week as I looked forward to this mission, I have been in hell. At last I said, 'Oh God, I cannot bear this any longer; I give in.' I wrote the letter, sealed it, and dropped it in the mailbox at midnight. As the letter went into the mailbox, heaven came back into my heart."

Of course it did.

What little thing is keeping heaven and God out of your heart, and all these blessings away from your soul? He is the One who brings the cleansing and the light, but you must be obedient. I ask you, look at that on which He has put His hand. Separate. Renounce sin. Step out upon God. Then healing and blessing will come.

Chapter 3

Naaman's Dilemma

"And there were many lepers in Israel in the time of Elisha the prophet; and none of them was cleansed, but only Naaman the Syrian." (Luke 4:27)

I thank God that the New Testament comes after the Old Testament, and that the words of Jesus light up for us that old-time story of Naaman the Syrian with great suggestiveness. From the words of the Master we find that Naaman had a second "but" in his life. We were introduced to the first one in the Old Testament, and it was full of sadness. He was a great man with his master; he was honorable; he was rich – *but* he was a leper! Now, Jesus says, *"There were many lepers in Israel . . . and none of them was cleansed, but only Naaman."* Naaman got into blessing. Naaman found a place where the leprosy passed totally out of his life. The sweetest word of all, it seems to me, in that story is – *his flesh was restored like the flesh of a little child* (2 Kings 5:14).

The law of life in the physical realm, as revealed in the healing of Naaman, is the law of life in the spiritual realm. The Master confronts all those afflicted with leprosy, the leprosy of sin; and He says to us, *"Truly I say to you, unless you are converted and become like children, you will not enter the kingdom of heaven"* (Matthew 18:3).

I do not intend to discuss the story of Naaman. It is familiar to us all. We know all its points and its beauties. My purpose is to find out how we can get the second "but" into our lives. We are all aware that the first "but" is there – at least, if we are not, we will never find our way to the second. We are all ready to say, "It is quite true that we have almost unnumbered blessings – health, reason, friends, and countless mercies; *but* we are sinners."

The supreme question for every one of us is, How can we experience the second "but," not theoretically, but actually, definitely, and positively, that it may also be said of each of us: *"But* he was cleansed."

There is a very terrible revelation in the word which Jesus utters about Israel: *There were many lepers in Israel.*

Lepers in Israel! Lepers among the children of the covenant! Men and women living right in the region of blessing and yet lepers. How absolutely and utterly useless was privilege to them, because they did not make use of it; because they did not take hold of the great blessing of God which was theirs as a nation and in the covenant, and appropriate it to themselves! Yet this man outside of the covenant; this man who had not lived in the realm of privilege; this man who had not been brought up in the knowledge of the revelations of God; this man who knew nothing in his family or in his history of the wonderful working power of the Most High; this outsider passed into blessing, while the men who were inside missed it!

The great truth that is impressed upon our minds from this thought is that it is not enough that you and I have been among the privileged people; it is not enough that we know the power of God; it is not enough that we have been brought up and nurtured in the fear of the Lord. There must be a personal appropriation of all the blessing presented to us in Christ, or else we miss the blessing: *"They will come from east and west and from north and south, and will recline at the table in the kingdom of God"* (Luke 13:29), while the children of the kingdom are *cast out.* It is not enough that we know these things; we must do them.

I want to say a word first about the need of every heart that has found the first "but" in their lives, and then a word about the message of the gospel to such needy hearts. And then I want to press home a final practical message.

I believe there is a general conviction of need. People generally agree that they need the pardon and the cleansing that Christ alone can bring; but I want, if I may, to analyze that general sense of need, and ask as through my own heart's experience, "What do I need?"

I answer it with three statements: I need something to be done about yesterday; I need something to be done about today; I need something to be done about tomorrow.

I need something to be done about yesterday, because yesterday was the day of sin. The years that have passed have been years of wrongdoing, actual wrongdoing, and years of carnal, self-pleasing rebellion against God. What am I going to do with these years? Suppose that I surrender myself to Christ, accept His invitation – what about the past? I need something to be done about the past, or else I can have no peace, no sense of purity, no blessing.

And then I know that something must be done about the present moment. Suppose it is possible to deal with the deeds of the past; I am still the same person, still in my own nature which will propel me to do wrong and to sin, and therefore I will still be unacceptable to God. I need forgiveness. I also need the consciousness of acceptance by God.

And then, after I have faced these two needs, if there is a message in the gospel that will meet my need about the yesterday of my life and the today of my life, I still have another need. I look to the future. I see tomorrow coming with the same temptations, the same suggestions to do evil, and I reverently say that if God forgives me of yesterday, and accepts me today, I am still helpless unless He makes some special provision for me tomorrow.

The general sense of the need is analyzed for my own heart when I take these three outlooks on my life – yesterday, today, and tomorrow. And what do I need? I need first of all pardon for the past; I need that in the present moment purity will be given to me so that my nature will be changed, and I will be accepted by God; and for tomorrow I need power for everything that will come. Pardon, purity, and power; pardon for yesterday; purity for today; power for tomorrow. I stand with the years of my life coming and going so swiftly that they seem to glide away before I know it, and I say, "In the past I sinned; I want pardon. In the present I am impure; can I have purity? And tomorrow – I dread it, because of my own weakness – can a power come into my life and energize me in the future?"

Now, is not this the gospel that you have heard your whole life? Is not every need that is expressed met in the message that Jesus Christ sends to you again today?

What about the past? He meets you at His cross and says to you, *"I have wiped out your transgressions like a thick cloud and your sins like a heavy mist"* (Isaiah 44:22).

Do you know what it is to wipe out a transgression? Do you know what it is to have sin put away at the cross of Christ? He did it with His own shed blood.

But what is this blessing of the blotting-out of sin?

A boy ran in to his mother one day after he had read that promise, *"I have wiped out your transgressions like a thick cloud,"* and he said, "Mother, what does God mean when He says, *'I have wiped out your transgressions'*? What is He going to do with them? I cannot see how God can really wipe them out and put them away. What does it mean – *wiped out?"*

The mother, who is often the best theologian for her child, said to the boy, "Didn't I see you yesterday writing on your chalkboard?"

"Yes," he said.

"Well, show it to me."

They went to his chalkboard. She pointed to it and said, "Where is what you wrote?"

"Oh," he said, "I wiped it out."

"Well, where is it?"

"Why, Mother, I don't know."

"But how could you wipe it out if it was really there?"

"Oh, Mother, I don't know. I know it was there, and now it is gone."

"Well," she said, "that is what God meant when He said, *'I have wiped out your transgressions.'"*

My friend, are you troubled about your past? Are past sins haunting you today? I am not asking you to list them – you cannot do it; but I ask you to remember that the list is made. The whole black list of sins is before you; and the Man of Sorrows and of tears, the Man of suffering and triumph is coming your way today, and He says, *"I have wiped out your transgressions."* He will put His own pierced hand on that list of your sins, and His own precious blood will cleanse the page of all your sins. It is His promise. He is able to promise this because He has been into the darkness of His death, and out of that darkness He brought authority by which He wipes out the sins of the past, and puts all of them away.

But I need more than that: I need purity; I need to know that I am accepted by God. And again He calls me to His cross, and at the cross He tells me that He will not only forgive my sins but also cleanse me from all unrighteousness. He tells me that He will take my nature, purify it, and make it like His own; and that in Him, and in the power of His life communicated to me, I will be accepted by God.

But how can I know this?

On His oath, on His covenant, on His blood I am to depend, and He says, *"The one who comes to Me I will certainly not cast out"* (John 6:37).

"Ah, but what about tomorrow? How am I going to manage tomorrow?"

The Master bends over the trembling soul that asks that question and says, *"Lo, I am with you always"* (Matthew 28:20).

Some years ago, in Scotland, a Scotch lord gave to his old servant Donald a little farm. He called him in one day and said, "Donald, I am going to give you that farm, so that you can work it for yourself and spend the rest of your life there on your own property."

Donald, with all the canniness that characterizes a Scotchman, looked up into the face of his lord and said to him, "It is not good to give me the farm; I have no capital to stock it."

His lordship looked at him and said, "Oh Donald, I think I can manage to stock it also."

And Donald said, "Oh well, if it is you and me for it, I think we will manage."

Trembling soul, if Christ Jesus pardoned you, if He purified you, then say to Him, "Now, Lord, I thank You for the pardon; I magnify You for the purity. But Master, I have no capital; how am I going to live in the future?"

And He says, *He who did not spare His own Son, but delivered Him over for us all, how will He not also with Him freely give us all things?* (Romans 8:32). *"Lo, I am with you always"* (Matthew 28:20).

"Jesus, Master, if it is You and me for it, we can manage."

So far, we have seen the need and the provision: yesterday, pardon; today, purity; tomorrow, power. The gospel of Jesus Christ is the same yesterday, today, and forever; pardoning the past, purifying today, and energizing for every moment of the pathway to glory.

Now we come to the point of actually dealing with God for ourselves. I cannot help you here, except to say what Naaman's servants said: "Try it." Even if you are very weak and trembling and doubting, never mind. Try it. Venture on God. Take some risk in the matter. Two men in the life of Jesus came to Him. We cannot read the story of either of them without sensing how poor they each were in faith.

One said, *"Lord, if You are willing, You can make me clean"* (Matthew 8:2).

Don't you see, he was not totally sure that the Master was willing, but he took a chance on Him. He came to Him on a crutch, and the crutch was a little *if – If You are willing.*

The other man had to get another crutch, a crutch for the other side, and he said, "If You can do something for my boy, do it." How did the Master deal with this man? Did He say, "No, I cannot help you; your faith is not strong enough; you don't have enough confidence." No, He did not. If a man came to Him, He did not care. It is better to come to Jesus with "Lord, You can," "You will," or "I believe"; but if you cannot come that way, come the other way. Come with your *if.* "Lord, if You can make me clean, do it; only I come to You."

Do you remember the four leprous men that sat in the gate of the city of Samaria? One of the most sensible committees that ever sat in the history of the world was that committee of starvation. There in the city of Samaria famine stared them in the face. The host of the besieging army had cut the city off from supplies. The committee of four lepers held one of the only committee meetings I would ever desire to attend.

I like to go there when I read about them and watch these men as they discuss the situation, propose a resolution, and carry it out. What is the resolution? They said, *"We will enter the city, then the famine is in the city and we will die there; and if we sit here, we die also. Now therefore come, and let us go over to the camp of the Arameans. If they spare us, we will live; and if they kill us, we will but die'* (2 Kings 7:4). That is the outlook: first, certain death in the city; second, certain death sitting here; third, half a chance of life down yonder. We will take a chance and turn our back on certain death in the city and certain death in the gateway, and will take the half chance of life down yonder."

Wasn't that a sensible thing for the committee to do? And you know how it worked. They took that half chance of life and found that it was not only a chance of life, but it was also more abundant life, life for everybody except for the men who did not believe that God could do it.

My friend, I want you to come to Jesus Christ that way now if you feel that you cannot come any other way. It is certain death to go back to your old life. It is certain death to sit in the gateway sighing for virtue and never finding it. You are not quite sure that Jesus can do for you what He has done for others, but you think He might. Then try Him on the off chance! Take a chance on Him. Come to Him now and say, "Lord, if You can do anything with the way I am – Lord, I give myself to You!"

How will it work? Many believers could tell you:

I came to Jesus as I was –
  Weary, and worn, and sad;
I found in Him a resting-place,
  And He has made me glad.

Accept that testimony. Come, take a chance on Him.

How was it that Naaman nearly missed cleansing? In 2 Kings 5:11-12 are stated two things that very nearly wrecked his faith. The first was: *"Behold, I thought"* – preconceived ideas of how God was going to deal with him; and the second was: *"Are not Abanah and Pharpar, the rivers of Damascus, better than all the waters of Israel?"* – an attempt to dictate terms to God as to how he should be healed. First, Naaman had an idea about how God should work, and because God was not going to work that way, he nearly missed his blessing. Then he wanted to say that he knew a better way – Abanah and Pharpar were better rivers than the muddy Jordan.

Thousands of souls have been wrecked upon one of those rocks at the entrance of the harbor of safety. *I thought* – what do you think? Do you think God will come and wave some magician's wand over you and give you some strange feeling? He never does. His way is the way of obedience. "Go to the Jordan and dip seven times! Go to Christ in absolute abandonment of yourself!" That is the only way to receive His blessing. And the only way in which some men and women will ever get through into salvation or sanctification is to sweep out of their life, by a determined effort of their will, all preconceived notions, and say, "Oh God, have Your way, in Your way, whatever I think."

The other danger is that we want to dictate terms. That is done so often. I remember years ago conducting a mission, and a man sat at the back of the chapel at the first meeting. After the meeting, as I moved around speaking to various persons, I came to that man. I found that the Holy Spirit of God had been dealing with him, but he looked at me and said (I had been inviting people to the counseling room), "Can't I be saved without going in there?"

Now, when a man begins to ask that question you must deal with him in just one way. I said, "No, I don't think you can."

"Why," he said, "is salvation in the counseling room?"

"No, it is in God; but just as long as you sit here and want to dictate terms to God, you are proving that you have not gotten to the end of yourself, and there is no salvation for you. That is the trouble with you."

"Then," he said, "if I cannot be saved without going into that room, I will go to hell."

"My friend," I answered, "that is not God's choice for you. If you have chosen it for yourself, I cannot help it."

Every night that man came and sat there. Oh, how gracious God is! He does not take us at our word. He does not leave us alone when we have said some rash, foolhardy thing.

I had warned the workers, and said, "Don't talk to that man. Leave him alone. Let God have His way with him."

I will never forget the last night of the mission. Before I had time to ask a soul to move, that man came forward over the backs of the seats to the altar. I looked at him and said, "I thought you were going to hell, my brother."

He said, "Oh, I have been there all the week."

Praise God! It sometimes does a man good to get there for a little while that way.

As long as you are dictating terms – "Can't I be saved right here?" – you are likely to miss the blessing. You *can* be saved there. You can be saved without anyone knowing about it at the time. Somebody is bound to know about it soon, however. Nobody ever became a Christian without it flaming out eventually. Nicodemus and Joseph of Arimathea both tried to be Christians in private; but later came the day of crucifixion, and

two men got the body of the dead Christ and laid it to
t rest. You cannot be a Christian and keep your candle
under a bushel for long; the light will either go out or set the
bushel on fire. You may think you can get to Jesus Christ quietly;
but as long as you are trying to dictate terms, as long as you
are saying, "I don't like this noisy, babbling, rushing, muddy
stream of Jordan; let me have the quiet, placid, sweet waters of
Abanah," you are not in a condition for blessing.

Rather, it is when you reach the point where you say,
"Anywhere that He points the way; any means that He says to
me; any cross that He puts in front of me, I will take that to get
to Him, to have His cleansing." When people reach that point,
then they are in the way of blessing. There were many lepers
in Israel, but none of them were cleansed except for Naaman;
and he was cleansed because he entered into the spirit of true
relationship with God by obeying. There are many who are
suffering from the leprosy of sin, but they, and only they, will
have cleansing who in the divinely marked way go to Him who
alone can cleanse, and abandoning all preconceived notions,
and sweeping aside every temptation to dictate terms, say,

> Just as I am, without one plea,
>   But – *(the best plea of all!)* that Thy blood was shed
>   for me,
> And that Thou bidd'st me come to Thee,
>   Oh, Lamb of God *(through doubt, darkness, difficulty,
>   in spite of obstacles!)* – I come.

God help us all to come!

Chapter 4

Do You Wish to Get Well?

*"Do you wish to get well? . . . Get up, pick
up your pallet and walk. . . . Do not sin anymore, so that nothing worse happens to you."*
(John 5:6, 8, 14)

It has been very beautifully said that all the parables of Jesus
are miracles of wisdom; that all the miracles of Jesus are
parables of teaching. Believing that statement is true, I propose
here to consider this miracle of healing as a parable of teaching.
In order to do this intelligently, let me remind you again of the
actual facts of the story from John 5.

Jesus had come up to Jerusalem, and passing through the
Bethesda porches, He had seen lying all around a multitude of
impotent people, sick, and maimed, and crippled, who needed
healing and deliverance. But the man who attracted His attention the most was the one in the crowd that badly needed the
most help. Christ is always primarily attracted by the neediest
cases. This man had been in the grip of his infirmity for thirty-
eight years. Now, that is very easily said, but not many of us can

know its actual meaning. Thirty-eight years of helplessness, strong enough now to be able to drag himself from the place where he lay in the porches into the pool; always longing to reach it, but always too late because someone else stepped down into the pool before him; and not able to persuade anyone to help him day after day, week after week, month after month; and still, when Jesus passes through, he is impotent and needy, and in all likelihood, frailer and weaker than he had ever been.

Now, think of the surprise of the whole story. There is no more dramatic incident in the New Testament than this. The crowds are thronging Jerusalem at the feast; the sick people are lying on all of the porches at Bethesda; and undoubtedly a great multitude of people are passing, as Jesus passed, through those porches. As the Master comes, His eyes rest upon this man, who lies there in all his need and in all his weakness; and looking down at him, He says to him, *"Do you wish to get well?"* And I can imagine the astonishment the man had as he looked up into the face of the Stranger.

Remember, the man did not know Him, did not know that it was the Prophet, mighty in deed and word, who was so strangely beginning to stir the whole country; and his very first word marks his astonishment – *Sir* – as though he had said to Jesus, What do you mean by asking me a question like that? – *"Sir, I have no man to put me into the pool when the water is stirred up, but while I am coming, another steps down before me."* Then Jesus said, *"Get up, pick up your pallet and walk."* I think a crowd gathered around them.

Human nature is the same in every age. They begin to watch and wonder, and I think, if I had been in the crowd, I would have protested against what Jesus had said. Here's why: while the crowd gathers, Christ quietly looks at the man, that man in the grip of an infirmity for thirty-eight years, so weak that he could not struggle his own way to the pool when the water was stirred, and he stands up, bends down again, picks up the bed that he had been lying on, rolls it up, flings it on his shoulder, and walks, a whole man, out of the porches that he had been carried into. And where is Jesus? He is gone. He walked away; the crowd was coming after Him and He left.

Now the man starts his walk home, and some of the men who were far more eager about the observance of the Sabbath than the healing of an impotent man stop him and say to him, *"It is the Sabbath, and it is not permissible for you to carry your pallet."* I like the man's answer: *"He who made me well was the one who said to me, 'Pick up your pallet and walk.'"* Then they said, *"Who is the man who said to you, 'Pick up your pallet and walk'?"*

You notice their question. They did not say, "Who healed you?" They were so concerned about the Sabbath. Oh, these men *who strain out a gnat and swallow a camel!* (Matthew 23:24) (who are concerned with something small and unimportant but ignore the large and important). *"Who is the man who said to you, 'Pick up your pallet and walk'?"* The man did not know that it was Jesus. He told them he did not know, so the questioning ended.

Now, in all probability – if I can follow up on the story, and I think I can do it correctly – he carried his bed home and put it down, left his house, eager and anxious to do what he had not been able to do for many years: mingle with the worshippers in the temple, go back to the temple courts, sing the songs of Zion, and go back to worship. And as he was there among the worshippers, moving around, probably greeting old friends, to their absolute astonishment, he suddenly stands again face-to-face with the Man who healed him. Jesus is in front of him. And Jesus looks into his face as he stands erect, and He says to him, *"Behold, you have become well; do not sin anymore, so that nothing worse happens to you."* And again, the Master leaves.

As far as we know, Jesus did not speak to the man again. But in those three things that Jesus said to him, I have a wonderful revelation of His consistent method of dealing with man. First, He got his attention, made him think, and appealed to his will: *"Do you wish to get well?"* Then He called him to act, to put into action the new awareness and passion that had filled his soul: *"Get up, pick up your pallet and walk."* And then, after he was healed, He told him how to live his life in a very simple law. He pronounced him well: *"Behold, you have become well"*; and then He gave him a commandment: *"Do not sin anymore"*; and then He lit for him a solemn and suggestive lamp of warning: *"so that nothing worse happens to you."*

Now, let's look at these three stages in the Master's method a little more closely.

Take the first: *"Do you wish to get well?"* The question is so simple that it seems as though we might dismiss it and not say anything about it. I am sure, however, that would be a great mistake, because the question that appears so simple is indeed sublime.

There are at least four facts within the scope of that question that we must examine, if we are to understand Christ's method of dealing with men. First, the Lord Jesus recognizes the royalty of human will (the right to make our own decisions; free-will choice). *"Do you wish to get well?"* And I say it very reverently, that unless a person does, Christ can do nothing for him.

But there is more than that in the question. Though it is not apparent in the question but is very evident from what followed it, there is a revelation to the man of his degradation. *"Do you wish to get well?"* The man's response reveals the fact that he never expected to be made well, that he had lost heart, that he had lost hope. He said, *"Sir, I have no man to put me into the pool when the water is stirred up, but while I am coming, another steps down before me,"* which, said another way, is, "It is no use asking me such a question; I do not have any chance of being made well." He had lost hope, and Christ's question revealed that fact.

Because Christ asked it, does not the question give a renewal of the very hope that the man had lost? The fact that the man answered him at all shows that suddenly there was springing up in the man's heart the hope that was dead. Why did he answer Christ? No, ask another question; ask the question that in all probability the man asked as he lay there: "What made this Man say that to me? 'Well' did He say? Why, there is the song of birds in the very word, and the breath of summer seems round about me once again. 'Well'? What does He mean? Is He going to do something for me? Is this the Man I have been waiting for, that will help me when no one else can?" And I think that while there is evidently a revelation of the degradation of the man, in that he had lost hope, there is also a revelation of the fact that the question renewed his hope.

And yet once again, there is not only the recognition of royalty of will, and the revelation of degradation, and the renewal of hope, but there is also for sure a requirement, a claim upon the man, in order to reach the end that is desired; it is the apprehension of the man, that the man may be ready for something else. If Christ stands outside that man's will, and asks that it may consent; and if Christ, standing outside the man, reveals the man's degradation; and if, in the very question, He renews his hope, then is there not a hint, an inference, a suggestion that if he is going to have any wellness that Christ can give him, he must be ready to do what Christ tells him? So it seems to me that we have at least four things revealed in this question.

When Christ comes to deal with a man that is impotent, a man that is in the grip of some mastering disease that is sapping his life and ruining his days, first He recognizes the royalty of human will; secondly, He reveals the fact of degradation, that hope is lost; thirdly, He renews hope by the very fact of His coming, and His question; and lastly, He requires submission to whatever He shall say, if the benefit that He is ready and willing to confer is to be obtained.

Now, for the moment, let us leave the story, and attempt to apply this revelation of its meaning to ourselves. If this study has any value in it, it has that value as we are conscious of our sin, conscious of our shortcomings, conscious that we are not what we would be, conscious of the passions that master us, of the evil things that hold us in their grip. If Christ is indeed to heal spiritually; if men are to lose the chains that bind them; if indeed "the pulses of desire" are to feel the touch of "His coolness and balm"; if the poison that has burned in our veins like a veritable fever is to be quenched, then there are certain things that we have to look solemnly in the face: things that are suggested by this very first question.

Jesus confronts you personally, individually, and in loneliness; and the question He is now asking you is: *"Do you wish to get well?"*

Now, let me say at once to you, that if you do not *wish to get well,* then I have nothing more to say to you.

I think we need to take these things step-by-step and be very serious about them, and businesslike about them. If there is a man who has no desire to be made well, no desire for pureness, no desire for wholeness, no desire for a higher way of life, no desire for the things that are beautiful, the things that are of a good report, then I have nothing more to say to that man. He drops out of my argument, he drops out of my message; I have nothing more to say to him. I have no authorization to deliver any gospel of power and of blessing to the man that does not want to be made well.

But listen now. Is there such a man? There may be, but I very much doubt it. I wonder if that statement sounds at all astonishing. I will repeat it, as revealing a growing conviction in my heart and life as I work for God, that you will have a very great difficulty finding a man that does not want to be made well. Oh, but you say, look at the men who are sinning, and sinning with a high hand and an outstretched arm. Look at the men that have all kinds of chances of changing. Look at the men who have heard the gospel message from childhood up, and yet continue to sin. Do you mean to tell us, someone is saying, that you think those men really want to be made well? In a vast majority of cases I believe they do.

I remember one early morning back in 1887. I had been out all night, sitting by the bedside of a dying man in Hull in the north of England. As I was going home after he passed away about four o'clock in the morning, I turned around a corner, and suddenly I came face-to-face with a young man, the son of godly people, a child of tender care and constant prayer, and yet who, having fallen into sin, was quickly sinking further into wickedness. Meeting him suddenly like that, just turning the corner so that there was no escape, he and I stood face-to-face. He was hurrying home through the gray morning, after a night of carousing. I took his hand in mine, and I looked into his face, and I said, "Charley, when are you going to stop this kind of thing?"

I will never forget it, I am sure, to my dying day. He looked into my face, a young man just about my own age at the time, and yet prematurely aged, with sunken cheeks and bloodshot eyes, and that gray ashen hue that tells of debauchery; and holding out a hand that he could not hold still, that trembled as he held it, he said, "What do you mean by asking me when am I going to stop? I would lose that hand here and now, if I knew how to stop." I do not think that was an isolated case. I believe that if you could get ahold of half these men that are going wrong, if you could only get ahold of them, and press them up into some corner in the early morning, catching them by surprise, when they are not prepared to debate with you or laugh at your question, they would speak out a great truth, and it would be: We want to be pure; we hate impurity.

Oh, I know you will suggest a hundred *whys*. Oh yes, I know all the whys, but face the fact first. I doubt very much if you can find me a young person who is playing the fool with himself, and sinning, sinning, sinning, but that if you could get under the exterior, if you could only know what is going on in his own heart, you would find a man who wants to be made well. I believe it profoundly.

Now, Christ asks first, that if that is true, if I am right about you, then will you say so to Him now? That is His first question.

But now, take the next step. This man did want to be made well. The question seems to be superfluous in one sense. I can imagine that the man might have said to Jesus, "Why do you ask me that? Do you think I love lying here? Do you think I am fond of this infirmity? Do you think that I really am happy with this destruction of my life?" The man did not say all that. What did he say? He said the next thing. He said in effect, "Sir, it is no use to ask me, I cannot be made well. I tried, but I never got down to the troubled water. I have been waiting for a man to help me; that man never came. It is no good, so do not ask me about being well. Of course I want to be well, but I never will be."

Now here we are touching the reason why so many of these men continue in sin. They have lost heart, they have lost hope, they do not believe they can be healed. When, every now and then, one of them comes to talk to me or some Christian worker, and the whole truth is talked out, in frankness, that is the story we hear again and again. A man says to us, "Oh, I would give anything if I could go right, but I cannot; it is no good. I have tried and tried and tried and failed and failed and failed. I have been to meetings, and I have been to ministers, and I have been to all sorts of people, and I have never yet been able to stand up and be strong, since I became the slave of sin." A man comes to me and says, "I am in the grip of alcohol." Oh, the number of such men that one must deal with. And he says, "I want to go right. God knows I want to go right, but I cannot."

Some years ago there was a man who was a member of my congregation, a man of means, a man who, every now and then, just broke out and simply went mad with alcohol. I went to see him as he was getting out of one of these terrible drinking binges, and sitting in his house with him, he looked at me with a sort of disdain in his face, the disdain which is the mark not of unkindness, but of inward agony, and he said, "Mr. Morgan, what is the good of your talking to me? You don't know anything about this passion for alcohol; you don't know what it means." He continued, "When the desire to drink hits me, if you put a glass of wine on that table, and standing on the other side of it you told me that if I touched it you would shoot me, and I knew that hell lay on the other side of the bullet, I would still drink that wine."

Now, if you do not know anything about it, do not think that that is fanaticism. There are many people in that condition. The grip of sin in the form of alcoholism is awful. When it gets hold of a man it becomes more than a spiritual sin; it becomes more than a mental derangement; it becomes a physical disease. Many people are in that condition, and they will tell you they have tried and tried and failed and failed. Don't they want to be right? Of course they do. What, then, is the matter with them? They have lost hope; they have lost heart. They are saying exactly what this man said: "There is nobody who can help me; don't talk to me about being well."

But what is next? And oh, friend, I am talking to you. God knows exactly what you are doing – nursing your agony, hiding your sin, hiding in the world from everybody except the Master.

Now, can I not say this to you, that just as Jesus' question suggested to this man another possibility, very faint, very unlikely, and yet something in it; and just as Jesus' question brought new hope to this man – can I not say to you that Christ's question should be, and I believe is, bringing a new hope into your life? You know that I want to meet you just where you are, friend, and help you. I want to meet you right down there in the midst of your weakness; I want to meet you with your underlying passion for wholeness, and your overlying conception that you can't have it; and I want to say to you, isn't the very fact that you are willing to listen, and that God's message is being delivered to you, and that once again the question of Christ is coming to you personally, *"Do you wish to get well?"* – is not there something in it that should at least suggest to you that there is half a chance, if not more, that Christ can do something for you? Oh, I will take you on your half chance, if you will only come, because my Master did.

I like to see the men that came to Him, being not quite sure that they would get anything, and yet they always got what they wanted. There was a man one day who came to Him and said to Him, "If You can do anything for my boy." It was a poor faith; it was a faith that came on a crutch – "If You can." Did Jesus say to him, "Well, if that is all your confidence, go away; if you question My power, I have nothing for you." No, no, Christ never does that kind of thing. If a man cannot come without his *if,* Christ will bless him, regardless of his *if,* if he will just come. Christ flung the *if* back at him, and He said, *"All things are possible to him who believes,"* and he got his blessing.

There was another man who came to Christ. This man did not say, "If You *can.*" The other man said, "If You *will.*" He did not question the power so much as the willingness. Jesus might have been offended, but did He send him away because he came with an *if you can*? No, oh no. He gave him His blessing. He said, "Do you doubt My willingness?" Listen. "I will; you are clean," and the man was clean.

So if you are coming with a crutch tonight, come. If you are coming tonight, saying as you come, "I don't think there is much in this; we have heard this kind of thing before," come. If you are saying, as many have said to me, "Oh, I have been in the counseling room before, never mind." Come on the half chance. Take your half chance. That is what Christ has come to do now, just to give you a gleam of light and a lot more than that. But that is the first thing. If you want to be made whole, I tell you that the fact that you are seeking light is a sign, or should be a sign to you, that there may be a chance, even for you.

Now, consider the last points: the royalty of will, the revelation of degradation, the renewal of hope, and the requirement of submission. Let me talk now as if I am the man himself who lies on the porch. He asks me, *"Do you wish to get well?"* Of course I do. He asks me, *"Do you wish to get well?"* What is the use, I cannot. He asks me, *"Do you wish to get well?"* He must mean something; obviously He means something. I am inclined to think that He means something. If so, I will have to do whatever He says. Ah, there it is. That is the last thing.

The question must come to that point. It is a wonderful question, one of Christ's questions, recognizing the man's royalty of will, standing outside him until he wants Him, and then flashing upon him his own degradation, and making him say there was no chance, and yet kindling in his heart the new passion for wholeness; and then suggesting, so that the man cannot escape the suggestion, that if this Stranger was going to do anything for him, then he must be willing to do what the Stranger tells him to do. So far it is all mental.

What is the next thing? Christ now passes from the realm of the mind into the realm of action, and He says to him three things: *"Get up, pick up your pallet and walk."* I do not want to insult your intelligence, and yet I want you to remember that He does not say, "Walk, pick up your pallet, and get up." You need to understand that. That is what some of you are trying to do. You are trying to walk before you get up. You cannot do it! Jesus began with the first thing, and then the second thing, and then the third thing. *"Get up, pick up your pallet"* – some of you would have left out the middle step; some of you would have said, "Get up and walk." Oh no, you will soon see the value of all three steps – *"Get up, pick up your pallet and walk."*

Now, what is the first thing a man must do if he is going to be made well? First, *Get up.* But what is that? What is the rising that this man is called to do? I ask that you notice very carefully what that is. It is the one thing that he cannot do, but that Christ tells him to do first. That is what made me say at the beginning of my message that if I had been in that crowd, I think I would have protested.

Let us go back, and imagine we are there. The porches, the sick people, this worst case of all. A Stranger coming through, suddenly stops and says, *"Do you wish to get well?"* and the man says, *"Sir, I have no man to put me into the pool when the water is stirred up."* And then the Stranger says, *"Get up."* Why, my friend, I would feel inclined to say to Him, "That is absurd; that is the one thing the man cannot do. Why do you suppose he has been lying here for all these years, if he could get up? Of course he cannot get up." I am prepared to say to this Stranger, first, it is impossible; therefore, it is unreasonable; and I am not going to change these decisions. Impossible, and unreasonable, and I utter my protest.

Why, what is this? The man is up! The man got up while I am arguing! Was I wrong to say it was impossible? Certainly not. Was I wrong to say it was unreasonable? Certainly not. But he is up. I know it, but he has done the impossible and the unreasonable thing.

That is the miracle of Christianity. That is the revelation of Christ's perpetual method with a man He is going to heal. Are you in the grip of some evil passion, of some evil habit? I ask you to notice that sin in every man focuses itself at some one point preeminently, and you know that you would have been in the kingdom of God years ago, except for one thing. You know what the one thing is, and when Christ begins to deal with you, He brings you face-to-face with your impossibility, and He says, "Now, begin there!"

To the young man who was a ruler, and wealthy, Jesus said, *"One thing you lack."* What was the one thing he lacked? Some men would have said it was poverty. But these are the men who do not read their Bibles carefully. What was it he lacked? Control! *"Follow Me."* But what was the hindrance between his life of self-control and his life of being controlled by another? What lay between the two? His wealth. Now, Christ said, *"Sell all you possess and give to the poor."* There was nothing more impossible in all that man's life than that he should part with his wealth, and Christ brought him face-to-face with his impossibility.

There was a man in the synagogue one day whom Jesus called out, and he came and stood in the front. What was the matter with that man? He had a withered hand. What will Christ tell him to do? Hold his other hand up? No, certainly not. What then? Hold out the withered hand, the one he cannot hold out! He always brings man face-to-face with the impossible thing. Always this, always this – the impossible thing!

My friend, Christ is not going to ask *you* to give up the drink. Certainly not. Why not? Because it is not your impossible thing. He is not going to ask you, my friend, to promise to stop swearing. Why not? Because you never do it. That is the human method. The human method is to get one, or two, or three little promises and try to make them fit everybody. And oh, how eager men are to give up their brothers' idols!

Oh, the difficulty of it, and yet the magnificence of it! Christ is dealing with every man alone right now, and you know what He is saying to you at your weakest point: Begin and do the right thing. *Get up!*

But now I say, while I am arguing, that the man has done it, and you may do it. Should we try and find out how this man did it? That is the great secret. There is no problem of such interest as to know how that man got up when he could not get up. I will tell you exactly how it happened, and I will tell you because I know, experimentally and personally, how it happened.

Let us look at it. Christ first addressed his will – *"Do you wish?"* That is the first thing. When Christ says, *"Get up,"* it means that His will is that the man should be made well. Now, remember another thing. There is power enough in Christ to make him well. Christ is quite able to supply him with all he needs. There is, however, only one way in which there can be a connection made between the power of Christ and the impotence of the man. The man cannot, Christ can. How are you going to join together the man's *cannot* and Christ's *can*? That is what we want to find out. When Christ said, *"Get up,"* the man said to himself, "I want to be made well, but it is no good; yet I wonder what this Man means. I will do what He says. I cannot, but I will, because He says so."

Now notice, Christ's will and the man's will touch, and in that connection, the connection of will with will, the power of Christ flashes into the man, and he stands erect, not in the energy of will, but in the energy of Christ, which has become his, because he has submitted his will to the will of Christ.

That is the way you will master that evil thing in your life, my friend, or you will never master it. It is the Christ-power that you need to set you on your feet and make you live. And you can only connect with the Christ-power when you will to do what He tells you to do. Oh, but you say, "I cannot." As long as you say that, you will not. But suppose you try another way. Do not say, "I will" anymore. You have said that many times and have been beaten.

Do not say, "I cannot." For as long as you say that you never will. What, then, should you say? Say this: "I cannot, but because He said so, I will!" You see in saying that, that there is an abandonment to Him, you are handing your life over to Him, you do it in obedience to Him; and whenever a man takes that stand, all the power he needs for the breaking of the chains that bind him are at his disposal, and he will stand up erect, able to do the impossible, doing by faith the unreasonable, because his abandonment of will and his act of faith have brought him into living contact with the Christ of God.

And now the man is standing up; what is next? *"Pick up your pallet and walk."* Pick up your pallet! I think one of the most illuminative and most beautiful things I have ever seen about that is from the pen of Dr. Marcus Dods, in just one quick sentence. Dr. Dods says, "Why was the man to take up his bed? In order that there should be no provision made for a relapse." Ah, that is the point. Did you hear it? I do not want you to miss it. No provision for a relapse. That is the principle upon which a man is to start his Christian life.

The temptation to this man was to say, "Well, I am up; I am up, really I am; yes, really I am up, and He has done it. But I think I'd better leave that bed; I don't know how I will be in the street; I don't know how I will be tomorrow. I'd better leave it in case I have to come back." Oh no, no, that will not do! Jesus said, "Pick it up, carry the thing that has been carrying you, master the thing that has mastered you. Pick it up! Pick it up!"

May I put the principle in other words, and say it this way: When you start to follow Christ, burn your bridges behind you! Do not give yourself a chance to go back. I do not think too much emphasis can be laid upon that. Oh, the people that leave the bridge, and presently slip back over it! Here is a man who has been, to revert to my previous illustration, the slave of alcohol. He says, "Now, I am going to quit this in the strength of Christ," and my profound conviction is that that is the only way a man can quit. "I am going to do it." He means it, and he gets up and starts; when he gets home, in some cupboard in his house is a half-bottle of whiskey.

What is he going to do with it? "Oh," he says, "I will drive the cork right in, and I will put a seal on it, and I won't touch it, but I will keep it in case I need it." I tell you, that man will want whiskey within twenty-four hours. No, no! If that has been your problem, when you get home, smash it, pour it out! I am not going to say soft, easy things. I am not going to tell you that all you need to do is believe. I want to tell you that you are to believe with the belief that manifests itself in works, and unless you have a belief like that, it is worth nothing. Burn your bridges, cut off your companionships, and say farewell to the men that have been luring you to ruin. Be a man, stand up, and say to the man that tempted you, and drew you aside, your dearest friend, "I am done, I am done; I am going the other way."

And I want to say this to you, that the chances are all in favor of the fact that the man will come with you. That is the remarkable thing about it, that the very man that is luring you to wrong will very likely come with you, if you are only man enough to burn your bridges. *Pick up your pallet and walk.*

And walk! I would like to tell you everything that is in that. But, I will tell you just one thing that is in it. Do not expect to be carried! Churches are way too full of baby-carriage Christians – men and women who have to be nursed and coddled by the ministers to keep them there at all; men and women who say, "If you don't call, then I am going." Oh, go! Give us a chance!

Now, if you are going to start to follow Christ, young man, young woman, my friend, my sister, then *walk*. And remember that when He gives you power to stand up, He gives you power to carry your bed after you walk – a great sufficiency of power.

Then Jesus met that man once again. What did He say to him then? *"You have become well."* Has He ever said that to you? No, someone says, I do not think He has. Then you are not a Christian. Do not be satisfied because someone else said you are well. Never rest until He has said it to your innermost soul and you know it. But when He does say it, then what? *"Do not sin anymore."*

Now, are you done with your argument as to whether or not you are compelled to sin? He says, "No." How dare you, child of His love, child of His blood, child of His power – how dare you go on sinning, and you say you can't help it, when He looks you in the face and says, *"Do not sin anymore."* He never says that to a man until He has made him whole. He does not begin by saying that. He does not go to the man that is impotent, to the man that is weak; He does not say tonight to the man that is outside the kingdom, *"Do not sin anymore."* He first heals him, He first gives him power, and then He tells him, *"Do not sin anymore."*

What else does He say? He says this: *"So that nothing worse happens to you."* What could be worse? To go back to your impotence, to go back to the old disease, and have no one come and heal you. That could be worse.

I leave you to follow the lines of that indefinite and solemn warning that Christ uttered to the man, but I pray that you will remember it. If you have been healed, if you have been made whole, if you have been born again, and you are playing with sin, and sinning on, excusing it as an infirmity, remember that Christ's word comes tonight, swift, scorching, scathing – *"Do not sin anymore, so that nothing worse happens to you."*

Where is my last word to be said? Back in the middle of the story. *"Get up,"* says the Master. Make a beginning, make a start, and make your start not by making up your mind that you are going to do great things, but by making up your mind that Christ is going to do great things, and you are going to let Him. That is the very heart of the message! That is the secret of power!

Chapter 5

Clay in the Potter's Hand

"Behold, like the clay in the potter's hand,
so are you in My hand, O house of Israel."
(Jeremiah 18:6)

This is, in the first instance, a national statement; but since the greater includes the lesser, we may argue that the principles which regulate national life must also influence individual life. The only social and national upbuilding possible must result from the upbuilding of the individual life and character. From this great national statement, made to God's chosen people, we will take the principle and consider it in its individual application.

Let us first examine the principle itself; second, our relationship to that principle; and third, the deep underlying truth which makes this principle one in which we may rejoice.

Look first, then, at this principle. *"Like the clay in the potter's hand, so are you in My hand, O house of Israel."*

Can anything convey the truth of God's sovereignty more forcibly and simply than these words? If you have ever seen clay on the potter's wheel, being molded and fashioned by the thought, will, and activity of the potter himself as the wheel revolved, you must have been impressed with the thought of surrender; for with no desire or suggestion expressed, the clay was yielded to the hands of the potter. It was plastic to his will and touch. God says, *"Like the clay in the potter's hand, so are you in My hand, O house of Israel."*

God has designed, created, and sustained me, and I have absolutely no appeal against His will. God has the supreme right to do whatsoever He wants with the earth, the nations, and each individual in the nations. If God chooses to mark a line and say, "There your service ends," do I have any right to complain? If God were to take me out of my present circumstances or out of this world today, no matter what use I have made of my opportunities here, do I have any right to complain or appeal against it? No. Whatever God chooses to do, He has the right to do. God has never ceded His sovereign right to the devil nor to anyone else. Though He still permits evil to exist in the world, He holds the reins, and the devil could not touch a single hair on the back of a single camel that belonged to Job until God gave him permission. God reigns! He is neither dead nor deposed.

The tendency today is to subscribe to a loose doctrine of divine government, which is producing irreverent blasphemy in the way that men look into the face of God and tell Him what He should and should not do. Blessed be His name that His ways are not our ways, neither are His thoughts our thoughts; for how many people would be stricken to the very death! How long-suffering God is! Clay in the hand of the Potter: that is our position, and He can make or break, mold or fashion us as He wills, so far as our right of resistance or questioning or complaint is concerned.

What is my relation to this great principle of divine

government? There is this difference between clay and myself: I have intelligence, and I have will, but my will is to omnipotence as the materialism of clay is to my will. Clay is infinitely below the potter and must submit to his pleasure. In the hands of God, I am even more powerless than clay in the hands of the potter.

What, then, is my relation to this principle? My proper attitude is to *acknowledge my weakness,* and to say that I have no power to alter my own shape or substance. What I am, I am, and out of that I can never be anything better. That which is flesh is flesh. That is my state by nature, and the part of wisdom is to acknowledge it and take that place before God.

The next step is to use that will that we talk so much about and act on the truth which Tennyson saw when he said,

> Our wills are ours, we know not how;
> Our wills are ours, to make them Thine.

We show our wisdom when our weakness is acknowledged by *yielding ourselves to God* and lying as plastic in His hand that He may work His will in our lives. There is to be perfect acquiescence in the will of God.

That is better than resignation, but there is something even beyond acquiescence: it is *delight* in the will of God. There must be no desire as to the shape I am to take, or to the manner of my preparation. We must be willing to let God work out His purpose in our lives by sickness, if He so wills it, or by suffering, by sorrow, by bereavement, by breaking us in order to make us. If I set my will up against that, then I am thwarting the Potter, and I am hindering His purpose. In brief, I must *abandon* myself to God. I must abandon myself to Him without questioning whether it is to be there or here, this way or that way, under these circumstances or those. The one question for me to ask must be, "What is Your will?" God is King, and I am to say amen to all His will.

Now look at the purpose of God underlying all His dealings with us. Put everything else out of sight. When we get to this point, though it be through heartbreak and disappointment, everything else vanishes from sight, and only the thought that God is doing a great work stands before us. We never saw this when God was dealing with us. At first, we simply stood in the presence of God and yielded ourselves to His will.

Underlying this is a deeper truth. It is contained in that old text which no preacher has ever exhausted, which every child loves; a truth contained in three short words; a truth which every child seems to feel, and which every aged saint confesses to have hardly touched the fringe of; a truth which holds all revelations and blessedness in it – *God is love.*

What has that to do with it?

Everything. I am clay in the hands of God, and I tremble; I am clay in the hands of love, and I trust. God is love. My creation is the creation of love. His purpose in creating me was love. His government is the government of love. He alone understands me and knows all my possibilities. I might live among you for years, and you would not know me. There are depths in every nature that no man knows. *No man hath seen God at any time* (1 John 4:12); it is equally true that no man has seen man at any time. We do not even know ourselves, but God knows us through and through; He understands our thoughts afar off, and there is no hiding ourselves from the searching of His eye. God is love, and consequently, when He surrounds me with law, it is love that surrounds me.

It is not a hard, unpredictable taskmaster that says, "Now that I have a being in my hands, I will enjoy having my way with him."

That is human. No, it is devilish! God says, "This is the child of My heart; this is the highest work of My creation, made in My image, and I will hedge him about with law and commandments because I love him and know all the depths of his nature. If I lead him through tears and suffering and sorrow, they shall be but the sweet ministers of My tender love and infinite compassion for him."

Love is on the throne. How can I learn that? By submitting to the kingship.

Many people have said to me, "We don't love God. We reverence Him and adore Him, but we do not really love Him. What should we do?"

My answer is: *"We love, because He first loved us."*

How do we find this out? Only as we face this first fact of His kingship and begin to obey Him. By obeying the law, a man discovers the love in the law.

Let me earnestly warn you against dividing God into halves and saying, "This is law and that is love." His law and His love are identical. A man should never talk about the providence of God as though it were a sort of afterthought by which He helps a man to bear the severity of law. God's providence is God's government, and no man ever passes into the realm of love until he recognizes God's kingship and submits at the foot of the cross to that kingship.

Take that exquisite teaching of our Lord when He says, *"So do not worry about tomorrow; for tomorrow will care for itself. Each day has enough trouble of its own"* (Matthew 6:34). He has been speaking to His disciples about food, and clothing, and the necessities of this life, and then He says, *"Your heavenly Father knows that you need all these things"* (Matthew 6:32). If I could see God as my Father, I could love Him. How, then, am I to come to see Him as my Father? What does Jesus say? *"Seek first His kingdom"* (Matthew 6:33).

You will find the fatherhood in the kingship of God, and the love of God in the law of God; you will discover the exquisite tenderness of the divine compassion when you submit to the sovereignty of God and yield yourself to His absolute control. How have I come to realize my mother's love for me and my father's love more than I ever could in my childhood? It has been by coming to understand that the very restrictions which they placed upon me when I was young were the restrictions of an intense love for me. I used to think they loved me when they let me have my own way, but I have discovered they loved me most when they did not let me have my own way. So we get an insight into the deep love of God by obeying the law of God, which at first seems irksome, and by submitting to this great supreme truth of the sovereignty of God.

God is leading you on and on, putting His hand on this and that, hedging you in here, and holding you up there; and it is always love that does it. There is always a more marvelous unfolding of His love in these acts of His, and you will only discover the love of God as your own heart responds, and as you submit yourself to His kingship.

Most reverently I take the supreme illustration of the love of God from the life of my blessed Lord Jesus. He said, *"I delight to do Your will."* And why? Because in His perfect, unquestioning obedience to the will of God, He knew what the love of God was.

All the divine blessings which we are seeking are conditioned upon this: that we recognize God's kingship, and submit to it really, absolutely, and with thorough abandonment of all questions. Some people tell us that we should always count the cost. We should, in everything except this. Here there should be no counting the cost; and by refusing to count the cost we count the cost in the best way; by refusing to attempt to reckon up God and ourselves by the puny laws of human mathematics, we reach the divine mathematics which take good care of us all the way and see to it that we abide in Him forever.

To rebel against this law is to take my life for a little while out of the hand of the Potter, and thus render it purposeless and shapeless, so that it becomes loss and ruin. To rebel is useless. God's law and righteousness are vindicated in human failure as well as in human success, and the man who shipwrecks is the man who, knowing the will of God, disobeys and goes out into the dark void where God is not. That man in his eternal loss vindicates the kingship of Jehovah. But, my brother, what God wants is your submission, because He loves to take you, perhaps to break you, but for your good; for I read that the potter broke the vessel on the wheel, *so he remade it*. The secret of all blessing is:

> I worship thee, sweet will of God,
> And all thy ways adore;
> And every day I live, I long
> To love thee more and more.

Chapter 6

The Divine Government
of Human Lives

*"The Lord our God spoke to us at Horeb, saying,
'You have stayed long enough at this mountain.'"*
(Deuteronomy 1:6).

The stopover of Israel, the ancient people of God, at Horeb had been important and interesting. There they had received from God the words of the law, the pattern of the tabernacle, and the ritual of worship. They had revelations of the glory of God there and revelations of their own hearts. They had found in themselves rebellion and sin, even in that brief time. They also had revelations of the tenderness and compassion of their God.

At last, the organization is complete; they are ready to move forward and take possession of the land which God has given them, and the word comes to them suddenly, with a pertinence that reminds them that in actual practice they are a theocracy under the direct government of God. Everyone holds to the theory of the divine government, but now a sudden order takes hold of the creed which they had professed and turns it into a fact to be put into practice. To these people stopping at the mount, in the place of revelation, in the place of wonderful blessing, the word comes swiftly and suddenly and startlingly: *"You have stayed long enough at this mountain"* (Deuteronomy 1:6).

This was indeed a startling and urgent word, revealing certain great truths concerning this government of God, which it is of the utmost importance that we should perpetually bear in mind.

It reveals to me, first, that *the divine government is a fact.* It also reveals certain truths concerning that divine government, namely,

1. That the divine government is a disturbing element in human life,

2. That the divine government is a progressive element in human life, and

3. That the divine government is a methodical element in human life.

If it is a fact that God governs my life and your life, then He will disturb us; He will disturb us so that we may make progress; and He will disturb us so that we may make progress along certain definitely marked lines.

First, these words reveal the fact of the divine government. How easy it would have been for Israel to settle down there and say, "We believe in God and in the divine government." Had there been no voice speaking to them in actual leading, no word coming to disturb them, they might have come to hold the divine government merely as a theory. Then it would have passed out of their lives and would have failed to be what it was intended to be to them.

Friend, let me remind you that the divine government is a very definite fact. God is absolute monarch wherever He is King at all. His government is autocratic. He does not consult with us about what He should do with us, where He should send us, or what He wants us to do. Moreover, His government is an imperative government. He never permits us to make compromises with Him for a single moment. He speaks the word of authority. He marks the path without ever consulting us, and having done so, our only relationship to that government is that of implicit, unquestioning, immediate obedience.

Now, consider what this government means. Imagine the stir that must have been created in that camp when the word came: *"You have stayed long enough at this mountain."* Imagine how tents would be lowered and camels loaded throughout the whole of the camp. The people who had been living there for a little more than a year were suddenly uprooted and ordered to move away.

Think of how, at the sudden proclamation of that word of God, all social and family arrangements had to be set aside. That word touched every tent and every soul, and wherever families had arranged to meet at a certain time for social gatherings, the whole plan was swept away. The divine voice had spoken, *"You have stayed long enough,"* and no engagement is of sufficient importance to hinder the divine word. Tents must be lowered immediately. All the minor arrangements of everyday life, important in their place, must be set aside, because the word of the King is supreme, and is sufficient in itself to set aside every arrangement that these people have made.

What a disturbing business! What a serious thing to be under the authority of someone who can upset everything in our lives without consulting us, and by a word can set for us the moment of departure! That is the government of God. We may talk and sing about the kingdom, and pray about the kingdom, but until we face that fact, we know nothing of what it is to be living in the kingdom of God and under the government of the Most High.

Human arrangements are constantly disturbed in the kingdom

of God, and what is more remarkable still, divine plans seem to change, and orders that we have most definitely received from on high are countermanded, and the whole program of life again and again is changed for the men and women who are in the kingdom of God and desire to obey only His will.

Today a man is in a sphere where God has put him, and on every hand, God is graciously setting His seal upon the work that He has given him to do. But the divine voice comes: *"You have stayed long enough."* That work must be dropped. All its hallowed associations must be left behind, and all the tender ties that have become entwined around the heart on account of that work must be snapped. The divine voice is heard – the only voice to which a man in the kingdom of God should pay any attention – and the sphere of work is entered into because the divine finger pointed that way must be left the moment that voice bids the man to move forward.

God comes into our lives in strange, mysterious ways when we are under His government. He may pluck away a loved one and leave us with broken hearts and almost desolate homes for a time. Earthly friendships are often severed by divine government. Two souls knit together in the sacred bond of friendship, seemingly created for mutual service in the kingdom of God, are taken by the divine government and separated by thousands of miles. Divine government is a disturbing element, breaking cherished plans, associations, and hopes. The aspiration of our heart, centered upon a friend, a child, or an event, is suddenly crushed, and in a moment, we find ourselves stranded in darkness! All this comes to men and women in the line of the divine government. It is a disturbing element in every human life. God has made His heroes and heroines by such dealings.

In Luke 12:35-36 we are very clearly shown the attitude of a Christian. *"Be dressed in readiness, and keep your lamps lit. Be like men who are waiting for their master when he returns*

*from the wedding feast, so that they may immediately open the
door to him when he comes and knocks."*

Here is the character of the Christian. *Be dressed in readiness;*
no settling down amid the things of the earth, but continu-
ally waiting for the divine voice; ready to be disturbed when
God would disturb; willing ever to respond to the expression
of the divine will and to be satisfied in obedience. Of course,
the ultimate issue of this is the waiting for the Master Himself
to come, but if I am living already dressed and waiting for the
last summons that calls me to fellowship in the ages beyond,
then I am ready for every call that precedes it, whether it be to
suffering or to service.

The same thing is taught by Paul in his letter to the Romans.
In Romans 13:11-12 he says, *Do this, knowing the time, that it
is already the hour for you to awaken from sleep; for now salvation is nearer to us than when we believed. The night is almost
gone, and the day is near. Therefore let us lay aside the deeds of
darkness and put on the armor of light.*

The scene is a military camp. Soldiers have been sleeping in
their tents, and suddenly someone yells that the day is breaking. Men get up and put on their armor, ready for the coming
of the king and his command. The awakening referred to here
is at the end of the dispensation, but it applies to our whole
life. Men and women who are under the government of God
are always homeless men and women, temporarily living in
tents, never living in houses. That is the character of the people
whom God governs.

But you ask, "Would you break down homelife?"

Of course not; but my home is to be where I live, and if God
orders me to tear down my tent and move, I immediately tear
the tent down and I move. See how Abraham, the father of
the faithful, lived. "A tent and an altar, a tent and an altar." He
pitched his tent and erected his altar. His altar was the mark

of the fact that he lived in relationship to the Divine. The tent marked the fact that he was only a sojourner, a stranger, and a pilgrim upon the road.

The divine government is a disturbing element. My duty is to live so that I will be ready to move at any moment God pleases.

Now look at the second point, because it explains the first. The divine government is not only a disturbing element in human life, it is also a *progressive element.*

God disturbs a man. Why? To move him on to something better – never that there will be retrogression, never merely for the sake of disturbance. If God asks me to tear down my tent today and move somewhere else, it is because somewhere else there is a higher possibility, a more glorious outlook, a more perfect sphere. I may not see the advantage at first, but God's eye is always on the consummation, and He moves His people step-by-step at the right moment in the right way, and ever, ever onward, towards that glorious consummation.

Progress is not necessarily pleasant. Notice how, years later, Moses spoke of leaving Horeb. In Deuteronomy 1:19 he says, *"Then we set out from Horeb, and went through all that great and terrible wilderness which you saw on the way to the hill country of the Amorites, just as the Lord our God had commanded us; and we came to Kadesh-barnea."*

That was the movement. But how? Through *that great and terrible wilderness.* It was not a pleasant experience, but it was progress; it was moving onward. It was a further march into the purposes of God.

Now, friend, if the divine government is a disturbing element, then to be undisturbed is to be God-forsaken. If we know nothing of the voice calling us to alter plans, set aside arrangements, and simply step out upon the divine word in faith as Abraham did, then we are God-forsaken men and women. Beyond that, to be God-forsaken is to settle for failure.

"Oh," you say, "let me stay here; my home is so comfortable,
I am so happy."

God says, "Move from this place and go there."

You say, "I cannot. Let me stay where I am."

What are you asking? You are asking for your own break-
down and failure. God's plan for you is progress and growth,
and you are asking for arrested development and failure.

"Oh no," you say, "I am only asking not to be disturbed."

It is the same thing. When you and I pray, in our foolishness,
that God will not disturb us, we are asking Him not to give us
progress, but to let us settle where we are and experience failure.

There is no more exquisite figure, I think, in the whole Book
of God of the disturbing element of divine government and its
issue than that in Deuteronomy 32. It is a beautiful picture. Read
verse 9: *"For the Lord's portion is His people."* This is exactly
what Paul says to the Ephesians about God's inheritance in the
saints. Very well, then. If the Lord's portion is His people, He
will value His people, and what will He do to them?

*"Jacob is the allotment of His inheritance. He found
him in a desert land, and in the howling waste of a
wilderness; He encircled him, He cared for him, He
guarded him as the pupil of His eye. Like an eagle
that stirs up its nest, that hovers over its young, He
spread His wings and caught them, He carried them
on His pinions. The Lord alone guided him, and
there was no foreign god with him. He made him
ride on the high places of the earth, and he ate the
produce of the field; and He made him suck honey
from the rock, and oil from the flinty rock, curds of
cows, and milk of the flock, with fat of lambs, and
rams, the breed of Bashan, and goats, with the finest*

*of the wheat—and of the blood of grapes you drank
wine"* (Deuteronomy 32:9-14).

That whole passage is full of exquisite beauty, but here is what
I want you to notice. Jehovah's portion is His people; where
did He find them? *"In a desert land, and in the howling waste
of a wilderness; He encircled him."* Then comes the verse that
reveals both the disturbing and the progressive elements in
divine government: *"Like an eagle that stirs up its nest, that
hovers over its young, He spread His wings and caught them,
He carried them on His pinions."*

That picture is full of poetry, full of life and truth and beauty.
Mark it. Have you ever seen an eagle stir up her nest? You know
what happens. There in the nest, right upon the rocky height,
are the eaglets; the mother eagle comes, and taking hold of
them, flings them out of their nest. They were so comfortable
there, but she flings them right out of the nest high above the
earth. They immediately begin to fall. They have never been in
the air before; they have always been in the nest.

Is not that mother bird cruel? Why does she disturb the
eaglets?

Watch her and you will understand. As long as you look at
the struggling eaglets in the air you will miss the point. Watch
the eagle. Having stirred up her nest, she spreads her wings wide,
the wings that beat the air behind her as she rises superior to
it. Where are the eaglets? Struggling, falling. She is superior;
they are falling. Then what does she do? She carries them on
her pinions. She swoops beneath them, catches them on her
wings, and bears them up. What is she doing? Teaching them
to fly. She drops them again, and again they struggle in the air,
but this time not so helplessly. They are finding out what she
means. She spreads her pinions to show them how to fly, and
as they fall again, she catches them again.

That is how God deals with you and with me. Has He been stirring up your nest? Has He flung you out until you felt lost in an element that was new and strange? Look at Him. He is not lost in that element. He spreads out the wings of His omnipotence to teach us how to soar. What then? He comes beneath us and catches us on His wings. We thought when He flung us out of the nest it was unkind. No; He was teaching us to fly that we might enter into the spirit of the promise: *They will mount up with wings like eagles.* He would teach us how to use the gifts which He has given to us, which we cannot use as long as we are in the nest.

Imagine the issue of keeping eaglets in the nest! It would be contrary to their nature, contrary to the purposes for which they are framed and fitted. There is a purpose in the eagle. What is it? To fly sunward. There is a purpose in your life, newborn child of God. What is it? To fly sunward, heavenward, Godward. If you stay in the nest you will never get there. God comes into your life and disturbs you, breaks up your plans, and extinguishes your hopes, the lights that have lured you on. He spoils everything; for what? That He may get you on His wings and teach you the secret forces of your own life, and lead you to higher development and higher purposes. This government of God is a disturbing element, but praise His name! it is a progressive element.

Now take the third point. Not only is the divine government disturbing and progressive, but it is also methodical. Tear down your tents, get away from this mountain. Where to? The land! That is the ultimate issue – possession of the land.

Now notice, beloved, that not only is there an ultimate issue in the mind of God when He disturbs His people, but there is also a clearly marked direction. We see this in Deuteronomy 1:7: *"Turn and set your journey, and go to the hill country of the Amorites, and to all their neighbors in the Arabah, in the hill* country and in the lowland and in the Negev and by the sea-coast, the land of the Canaanites, and Lebanon, as far as the great river, the river Euphrates."

There is direction towards possession.

But the most exquisite statement of all that marks the divine arrangement for the journey is in verses 32-33: "The Lord your God, who goes before you on your way, to seek out a place for you to encamp, in fire by night and cloud by day, to show you the way in which you should go."

Did you ever read anything more beautiful than that? It is one of those things that absolutely masters me. God going in front; what for? To choose a place for them to pitch their tent. They have torn down their tents, given up their plans, and are obedient to the disturbing voice of His government. Then what does He do? He goes in front and shows them the next place. At nightfall, the cloud stands still and changes into a pillar of fire, giving them light.

There is nothing haphazard or accidental in such a life. God's people move in a plainly marked pathway, step-by-step. The government of God not only disturbs them, and disturbs them for progress, but it also disturbs them for every inch of the way that He has arranged for them.

O friends, as we ask you to submit to the government of God, remember this: God is not experimenting with you. We are not pawns moving on a chessboard which God may win or lose. Every move is arranged. I did not know what would happen today, but God knew this day before I got to it. What was He doing? Choosing the place for me, making arrangements, and controlling everything. If your life is under the divine government, do not forget that every day you live God has been preparing for you. Do you believe it? Is God sending you to some foreign land? God is there getting ready for you to come. God goes in front as well as behind me. He is my rearward, but He is also in front, choosing, selecting, planning, arranging everything for me.

It is something to be thankful for, then, if God is disturbing me so that I may progress, and if He is always marking the path before me. There can be no accident to that man. Nothing can go wrong in the life surrendered to such a divine government. It is a disturbing element, a progressive element, and yet, thank God, it is a government that makes no experiments, but that moves along lines of perfect order.

Now, what is my relation to this government of God? I can put it simply: First, I should always be ready; and second, I should move the instant I am told to move. That marks the line of wisdom. Ready to be disturbed if God disturbs; immediate obedience when He calls.

Now I do not think that anyone can possibly say, "But that is very hard." It would be hard if we did not know God, and if we did not know that the disturbance is for progress, and that the progress is along lines definitely marked out and divinely arranged. Oh, the inexpressible comfort, the absolute rest of life for men and women who say, "If God disturbs me tomorrow, then being disturbed is my chief rest, because I know that when He moves, it is to reach higher in life, to go to better positions; and though the ultimate issue of this present disturbance may be long, every mile of the journey He has chosen, and every place where I pitch my tent He has selected for me."

That is the kingdom in which I want to live; that is where I want to always abide. I want to be a man waiting for the disturbing element, responsive to the progressive element, rejoicing in the methodical element by which God leads me day by day and hour by hour.

And, beloved, how do we mark our folly? By doing just what Israel did. They were characterized by wisdom at first. They tore down their tents and moved, but then they reached the borders of the land that God had told them to go in and possess, and then they began to doubt the King; they began to wonder whether He knew His business. When they reached the borders of the land, they said, "We will send men in to spy out this land."

When the men came back with the report that there were giants and walled cities, those who up to that point had been responsive to the divine government said, "Ah, well, you see God did not understand this when He sent us here. We cannot go on. He did not know that there were walled cities; He had no idea that there were giants."

Did they not say that? They said, "*We* had no idea," which is the same thing. If they had believed that God knew, and that He had been moving before them, choosing the place, then what would they have cared if there were walled cities and giants? Some of you have obeyed so far. God has said to you, "*You have stayed long enough at this mountain.*" He has broken up your nest somewhere. You tear down your tent and start; but there comes a moment when you say, "But somebody told me that there are giants and walled cities ahead."

So there are, it is quite true; but the giants are for you to kill, and the walled cities are for you to live in. The God who disturbed you did it so that you might come into possession of that very land; and if you live in His government, rest assured that for every step of the way that lies ahead, He will move before you, and choose the place, and equip you for life and for service.

But it was a very sad situation for these people. They disobeyed God and were sent back. What then? They thought they would go and try by themselves. They were defeated and driven back, and for nearly forty years they had to stay in that wilderness instead of immediately possessing the land.

Now, in conclusion, I want to ask this one pointed question of my own heart and of yours: Where do we stand in relation to this government of God? You may have just heard the voice saying, *"You have stayed long enough at this mountain,"* and He charts for you a new course of life. It is as clear as the sunlight in the blue. Wherever there are hearts waiting for the voice of God, that voice is to be heard. You know what God wants you to do. Now, what are you going to do? I beg of you for your own sake, as well as for the glory of the kingdom of God, that you do not stop to count the cost of obedience, but that you say, "He asks me to go, and I go."

That is the spirit which has brought men into the places of heroism and victory.

You know the old story of Luther; when he was warned against going to Worms, he said, "Though every slate on every house were a devil, I would go."

God had marked the path, and he was bound to go.

If you begin to count the cost, you are in the place of peril. It is the man who says to the King, "At your word, O King, in the face of what seems to be a combination of circumstances that will wreck me completely, I will go." You do not need to fear, for He goes before you to select a place in which you can pitch your tent, and the life abandoned to God is in perfect safety forevermore.

But perhaps you heard that voice speaking to you years ago, and you disobeyed, and you have been in the wilderness ever since. You have been away from the land towards which God was sending you forward to possess. Thank God, He is full of tender compassion and graciousness. All He asks is that you go back to the point of disobedience and obey. God's path led that way, and you turned from it; go back. You know how you got off the definitely marked pathway and missed the place that God had chosen for you to pitch your tent. Go back, friend, and go along that path.

But you say, "That path is thorny and rough."

Trudge on; for, be sure of it, you will find that whenever you step on a thorn, another foot has already been there and taken off the sharpness; and whenever you begin to trudge on a rough piece of road in obedience to the divine voice, another by your side will take the roughness from it, and you will simply walk in perfect harmony with Him who is your perpetual companion in the way of His own choosing. God not only goes before me to choose a place for me, He also walks with me along the pathway, and when I lean on His strength, then am I strong.

One word more. There may be some to whom all this is as a foreign language. You have never heard the voice of God. You say, "The day of miracles is past. I am never disturbed. I make my own plans and live where I please and do as I like. What do you mean by a *disturbing element*?"

Friend, you are still living among the fleshpots and the garlic of Egypt. You are still in slavery. Oh, if men could but see themselves! The man who does as he likes is the greatest slave. The man who never does as he likes is God's free man. You know no disturbing voice? God never points out for you a pathway altogether different from the one you had planned? Then, my friend, you are living still in the land of slavery, in the land of darkness. Go back to your King! In His government alone lies safety; in His government alone is the place of life, and light, and liberty, and love. Any man who lives outside this government of God is in the place of dust and ashes and emptiness. Oh, go back to your King!

Men, women, brothers, sisters in Christ, those of you who have never yet submitted to Him, come under His control actually and positively. Throw away your theories and get into the reality of this business, and let God govern your life, disturb you, chart your progress for you, and prepare for you your sphere of service. He will call you away from some loved relationship, from some cherished habit, and will say, "This is the way." As you look at the pathway, you will think that it is a hard one; but as you begin to walk it, you will find that He is with you, and is leading your every step into finer air, larger life, and more infinite possibilities.

Chapter 7

Redeeming the Time

*Therefore be careful how you walk, not as
unwise men but as wise, making the most of
your time, because the days are evil. So then do
not be foolish, but understand what the will of
the Lord is. And do not get drunk with wine, for
that is dissipation, but be filled with the Spirit.*
(Ephesians 5:15-18)

These verses form the setting of a passage which is full of
value in revealing the responsibility of Christians: *making
the most of your time, because the days are evil.*

Instead of *making the most of your time,* another way to say
it is "buying up the opportunity." That is a clearer translation of
the original word; and I intend to use it to convey the thought
in the mind of the apostle: buying up the opportunity, because
the days are evil.

Buying up. The words so translated come from another word
which means "the marketplace." In rural districts the market
is often held on one day of the week, somewhere in the center

of the town, sometimes undercover, sometimes in the open; and people who have goods to sell and people who want to buy come to that common meeting place, and there they transact their business.

In Eastern towns the same activity happened. The merchant-man came to the marketplace in the center of the town, bringing his goods with him, to transact his business there; and he watched the market, and waited for a favorable opportunity, either to buy or sell, and when the opportunity presented itself, he acted quickly. He bought up his opportunity.

Now, the apostle tells those who are the children of God to buy up the opportunities, because the days are evil. You cannot read the epistles of Paul carefully without noticing how he never forgets the relationship that exists between doctrine and duty. He perpetually lays down for us great principles of life, and unfolds before us the great truths of the gospel of Jesus Christ. But he never does so in order that men and women may possess the knowledge merely as theorists – he always does it in order that he may lead them to a practical application of the truth he declares. The apostle never forgets that the wonderful sanctifying force is the force of truth. Take his epistles and look through them, and you will find invariably that there is a statement of some great doctrine, and then you come to the point in the epistle where he uses his favorite word, *Wherefore,* and from that point he begins to apply his doctrine to the details of daily life.

This epistle to the Ephesians may well be spoken of as the epistle of vocation. In it the apostle unfolds the truth concerning vocation, and then endeavors to set the Ephesians' eyes upon God's ultimate purpose for them; and when he has done so through the first and second and third chapters, you find that the fourth chapter opens this way: *Therefore I, the prisoner of* the Lord, implore you to walk in a manner worthy of the calling with which you have been called.

The vocation is declared in the opening part of the epistle. The effect that the holding of the truth of that vocation would have upon daily life is declared later in the epistle. Paul begins by taking us to the heights of vision; then he brings us to the everyday level of life, and shows us how the vision, unfolded before us, should affect us as fathers, and children, and leaders, and workers.

A charge has been made against certain ministers in recent years that their preaching has been "otherworldly." The moment the church of Jesus Christ ceases to be otherworldly, she loses her power to affect this world. It is only in proportion to our true view of the heavenly calling that we are able to touch the earth that we live on, as men and women of power. It is only as we realize that everything that happens to us in the short time between our conversion and the coming of Jesus Christ, all the service rendered and all the lessons learned, is to prepare us for the higher service that lies beyond, so that we will always be able to give service at its fullest and best upon this earth. I live on that opening because it lends force to the present duty as laid down in this verse: *making the most of your time, because the days are evil.*

This first thought must be the very background of all our study. Paul, in these opening chapters, has written down the great truth that the church of Jesus Christ will only reach its full sphere of service when it has left behind it the temptation, and the sin, and all the various experiences of these passing years. Not today can we give our full service, but in God's great tomorrow, when (as Paul shows in this epistle) the church of Christ, the universal church, the church redeemed out of the earth, gathered into eternal union with Christ in the heavens, has become the minister of the grace of God to the ages that are yet unborn; a medium through which God will unfold in perfect clearness to principalities and powers in the heavenly places His own wisdom and His own power.

We are a heavenly people living on the earth; therefore, through us, the light of the heavenly is to fall upon the earthly. The powers of the world to come are to touch the present age through the men and women who are sons and daughters of the world to come, and who will only find the fulfillment of their highest vocation when that eternal day breaks beyond the mists and beyond the shadows.

Now, with that thought in mind, remembering that we are a heavenly people called to work in the heavens, how are we to act upon the earth? The second half of the epistle answers the question. I choose to take from it this one phrase, expressing our present duty and privilege: *Therefore be careful how you walk.* Note the connection with the opening injunction in Ephesians 4:1 – *I . . . implore you to walk in a manner worthy of the calling,* and then in Ephesians 5 – *Therefore be careful how you walk, not as unwise men but as wise, making the most of your time, because the days are evil.*

Notice, first, the reason that Paul gives why Christian men and women should buy up the opportunity: *because the days are evil.*

Now, if we had come into Ephesus as it was then and told the leading men of the city that they had fallen in their lives upon evil days, they would angrily have resented the charge. They would probably have said, "Ephesus has never seen such a time like now. We have never been so prosperous as we are today. We have never been as wealthy as we are today. Progress has marked the past, and today we are rich and wealthy."

At that time there was a very peculiar combination in Ephesus. Commerce and religion had been united – that was, of course, the religion of Ephesus. The great temple of their worship was also the banking house of the merchants, and as the merchants poured their wealth into the temple for safe custody, that became an act of worship. Men were perfectly satisfied with themselves in Ephesus, and thought it was a day of prosperity and a day over which they could rejoice; but Paul was writing not to the citizens of Ephesus, not to the rank and file of the people who lived there, but to the church of Jesus Christ, to the children of God, to the men and women of heavenly vocation; and writing to them, he said, *The days are evil.*

So they were. They were evil to the men and women who had turned their backs to idols to serve the living God. The prosperity of Ephesus was the adversity of the church. That which the men of Ephesus boasted about made the days evil to the called-out, separated, sanctified men and women whom God was preparing for the high vocation that lay beyond, in the heavens.

The apostle said to these people, "You are to buy up the opportunities." This great message comes to us. Our calling is a heavenly calling. The life of Christ, bestowed in conversion and coming into us in all its fullness in the moment when we fully surrendered to Him, subduing us unto Himself, is preparing us for the high calling that lies beyond. For us today the word to us is that we are to buy up the opportunities, and just as surely as the apostle said to these people of Ephesus, *the days are evil,* the days are evil for us, too.

Now, in what sense are the days we live in evil days? The world is perfectly satisfied. We are constantly being told there never was such an age as this – an age of progress, an age of advancement, an age of enlightenment. There was a danger of some men dying of pride before the last century ended, because it had been such a wonderful century. The dawn of the new century has increased rather than diminished that pride. Our cities have marks of progress on every hand. Our commerce is more wonderful than it ever was, and throughout the land you hear the voices of men and women telling you that these are the best days, days full of hope characterized by progress, days in which the race may be perfectly proud of themselves; and yet in these days the message comes to us: "Evil days!"

Now analyze that thought for a moment or two. The majority of the men with whom you come into contact in ordinary business life are not godly, but ungodly. You are bound to mix with them, as matters stand in our cities and in our daily life today. Please do not misunderstand me. I do not say that these men are all disreputable, or wicked, or fallen.

Never forget that a vast amount of the ungodliness of this age, as of every other age, is cultured and refined; but it is nonetheless ungodliness. You can have an ungodliness which is educated, and cultured, and refined, and accomplished, but it is still ungodliness – and I say the majority of the people with whom you come in contact daily are ungodly people. The days are evil days, then, in that sense, for the development of Christian character.

Take the activities of your own life for a single moment in this age when we have gotten away from simplicity, when we are living a terribly complex life. Did you ever try to see how little you could live on for one single week in your life? Did you ever try to discover how you are almost compelled by the very character of the age in which you live to give hours of thought and attention every day to an enormous number of things which you could very well do without – material things all of them, with no touch of spirit in them? What should we eat? What should we drink? What should we wear? These are the questions that we face today, in a number which our ancestors did not have to face. All this is far from being helpful to spirituality. These are evil days.

Then we are told that this is the age of progress. It is the age of rush, of movement, of effort. The old sacred art of contemplation and meditation is almost dead. It is the age when men and women are trying to live, even within the church, by degenerating and exciting forms of so-called religious services. The old solemn hours of quiet aloneness with God that made the saints of the past, are almost unknown. We are carried up and borne forward before we know it, upon the rush that characterizes the times.

Oh, when men and women come to me, as they do sometimes, and tell me, "What we need in the church is just to catch the spirit of the age and keep level with it," I say, "In God's name, no! What we need is to be led by the spirit of God, and that will send us against the spirit of the age, and never along with it."

All the rush and restlessness of the age that have crept into the church of Jesus Christ mark these days as evil days.

The general atmosphere in which we are surrounded is against the government of God. Do not let us deceive ourselves. Do not let us have meetings and sing the praises of what we have done and where we have reached. I tell you that if Jesus of Nazareth came back to London and preached the gospel that He preached in Jerusalem, they would crucify Him quicker than they did in Jerusalem. If He came again with the same words, the same teaching, the same actual statements of divine will and government, He would find no room for Himself in the very cities that bear the name of Christian today.

I repeat that the very atmosphere in which we live is against the government of God; and the most terrible thing is this: that while men are against the government of God, they are praying, "Thy kingdom come; Thy will be done." The most terrible blasphemy of the age is not the blasphemy of the slums, but the blasphemy of the temple, and the church, and the place of worship, where men pray these prayers and then go out to deny every principle of divine government in their lives. And

Christian men and women are living in the midst of all this, and the message that came to men at the church at Ephesus is the message that comes to us: "Buy up the opportunities, because the days are evil."

Now, do you see what the apostle says? He says that the fact that these are evil days is something which positively creates our opportunities. All these contrary facts are to be treated as opportunities for accomplishing the business of God. God calls you, God calls me, God calls every child of His to be His representative in the world, taking hold of the things that seem to be against the development of spiritual character, and turning them into opportunities for accomplishing His work upon the earth.

And when we have said all we could have said concerning the days, we have simply laid down the foundation upon which we may build for God. We have simply stated the opportunities which throng upon every side for doing His business and buying up the opportunities for Him.

Take any of those I have spoken of. Do I say that the majority of the men that you are surrounded by every day are ungodly men? Every ungodly man that you do business with is an opportunity that you may buy up for God, if you will, an opportunity for the display of your godliness upon his ungodliness.

But you ask, "How do we do it? We have no time to talk to these people about religion."

I will not say anything about that. I personally believe that the gift of personal dealing with men and women is a great gift to be earnestly coveted; but apart from actually saying words, for which I am not pleading for the moment, if you are a truly godly man, your godliness will reveal itself upon ungodliness without your saying a single word. I am not saying that businessmen should always put tracts into their letters, or anything like that, but I am asking that the businessman remember this:

"I belong to the heavens, and when I touch the earth, I must touch it with the equity of the heavens.

When I sell products, I must bring into my transaction the righteousness of the heavens. If I sell a certain measure over the counter, I must remember that the God of the heavens to which I am going for higher service hates an unfair measure and an unjust scale; and into every transaction of my business, I am to bring the principles that make the foundation of the heavens of God. I must bring into all those transactions the principles of righteousness upon which God is building His city and accomplishing His work. I am to make a name for Jesus Christ in my business. I am to run my business among ungodly men so that they will say, 'You can trust that man because he is a Christian.'"

There will be a great revolution before that day comes. Sadly, people do not say that now. And we – because we have labeled men Christians who are not Christians; because we have said these men are God's own children who are not His children; because we have a false label on the nation, and a false label on men, and a false label everywhere – are causing the very name of Christ to be blasphemed. What we need is for the true children of God – the members of the church with the light of the heavenly calling upon them – to take hold of ungodly men, and look upon them as an opportunity for influencing them by the godliness of their own lives.

So it should be with the activities of life. Jesus Christ was no monk. No Christian has any right to attempt to create saintliness of character by hiding himself from the activities of everyday life. No. I must live in my home, but that home must have upon it the stamp of the heavens. I must mingle with my friends, but my contact with my friends is to be that which will draw them towards God. I remember very well when I was married, my father came into my home. He was a Puritan, and

I used to think that he was hard-lined, but today I thank God for it. He came into my home soon after I was married and looked around. We showed him into every room, and then, in his own peculiar way, he said to me, "Yes, it is very nice, but nobody will know walking through here whether you belong to God or the devil."

I went through and looked at the rooms again, and I thought, "He is so right," and we immediately decided that there would not be any room in our house that did not have some message – in a picture, or a text, or a book – for every visitor, that would tell them that we serve the King.

It is our privilege to take the home in which we live, all of our activities, and turn them into opportunities for displaying godliness. We should take all those things and let the light of the heavenly fall upon them; we should go through life showing how all the things of the earth can shine in new beauty as the glory of the heavens falls upon them. Everything in life is to be an opportunity for accomplishing the business of God.

The unrest of the present age we live in is a glorious opportunity for displaying the quietness and the calmness of the secret place of the Most High. Oh, for quiet men and women, men and women who know how to be at peace amid the strife! We know a few.

That man who, whenever he walks into a committee meeting, brings heaven's calm with him. His words are few, but his presence speaks. As he enters, you feel that you are coming into contact with one who, amid the rush, and the bustle, and the hurry of a godless age, dwells in the secret place of the Most High, and abides under the shadow of the Almighty. A blessed thing it is to have men and women who have learned the secret of quietness, and so buy up the rush of the age and turn it into displaying the peace and the quietness of God!

But if I am to take all of life in this way, if I am to seize these opportunities as they arise and turn them into account for God, there are certain facts that I must bear in mind: the responsibility that I have to see the opportunity in the first place; and after seeing the opportunity, that I am willing to make some sacrifice in order to possess it; and that if I am to see an opportunity and make a sacrifice in order to possess it, I must always maintain a right attitude before God, always living in the power of the heavenly calling, and allowing Him to have His way with me and do His own work through me.

Now there are three laws revealed in the surrounding verses which set forth the conditions for the accomplishment of this business of the heavens. Let me very briefly point them out to you.

The first law is in verse 15. Men and women who are going to do God's work, *Therefore be careful how you walk. Walk circumspectly,* as the King James Version has it. Look carefully at how you walk.

My dear friend, you cannot do God's work in the world, buying up opportunities for Him, transacting His business, if you are careless and indifferent about it. *Be careful how you walk.* I know men and women who are very careful when they are at home, and awfully careless when they are away from home. I know other men and women who seem to imagine that they can live the Christian life and do God's work without being careful in the small details of everyday life. If I am to translate my life into service for God, not merely in the deeds done in connection with the church, but also in all hours, I will only do it as I live carefully day by day.

That word *circumspectly,* what does it mean? Let me give an illustration, which I believe originated with Mr. D. L. Moody, which is very quaint and forceful of what it is to walk circumspectly.

You have sometimes seen the top of a wall covered with mortar, and in the mortar pieces of glass are stuck all the way along it to prevent boys from climbing and walking on it. You have also seen a cat walking on the top of that wall. That was walking *circumspectly*. How the cat picked its way! With carefulness it put down its foot every time. It made progress by walking very carefully and looking for each place to put its foot among the pieces of glass.

You and I must walk like that if we are going to do anything for God in the world. You cannot go through a single day carelessly and let things go as they will. Every step must be watched. Every moment must be held as sacred for God, and we must always live in the power of the thought that we may miss an opportunity. We must take every moment as an opportunity that needs watching and buying up carefully. We must walk circumspectly.

The second law of this business of God is found in verse 17: *So then do not be foolish, but understand what the will of the Lord is.* That is to say, if I am to do this business of God as a Christian man, I am must not only be careful about it, but I must also have keenness and shrewdness. I must know the will of God. I must form the habit of discovering the will of God.

You remember that wonderful word about the Messiah uttered by Isaiah long before He came: *And He will delight in the fear of the Lord* (Isaiah 11:3). One Bible student says this might be rendered, "He shall be keen of scent in the fear of the Lord" – discovering the will of God quickly by a kind of intuition.

You only discover the will of God as you obey it the moment you discover it. It is in proportion as I walk carefully, obeying the will of God as it is unfolded, that I become quick to discover the will of God. We are not to foresee; we are to understand the will of God. We are to be a people shrewd, keen, having in our Christian life – having in our accomplishment of this work of God – a spiritual insight which is as necessary as business insight is to the man who is going to make his fortune in business.

And then there is the third thing. I must not only be careful, shrewd, and keen in understanding the will of the Lord, but I must also have capital, or I can never do God's work in the world. I cannot be a merchantman for heaven unless I have heaven's capital, and here it is in verse 18: *And do not get drunk with wine, . . . but be filled with the Spirit.*

When a man is filled with the Spirit, he has the capital of God to do the work of God. Then everything that I have said will become easy and natural. It will become – I was going to say second nature, but I will say something better – it will become first nature. It will be perfectly natural to influence men toward God.

This great subject of influence we have heard about since we were children, but we have hardly begun to understand or explain it. We have never seemed yet to grasp this truth, that the influence a man exerts is the influence of what he actually is in himself. You talk about keeping up appearances. You talk about living properly before men. You say, "Well, I wouldn't like to do this, that, or the other before people, because I must keep up an appearance or I will lead them wrong." It does not matter.

Do what you are, because whether you do or do not, you will influence men by what you are. Influence is altogether too subtle to be changed by any outward activities. If a man is filled with the spirit of God, he is spiritual, and his influence will be spiritual.

Some years ago I was at work in Hull, England. God was giving us gracious seasons of refreshing, and a man came to me one night and said, "Do you know, the strangest thing has happened to me!"

I said, "What happened?"

He said, "I am a cabinetmaker and I work at a bench. Another man works next to me. He has worked next to me for five years. I thought I would like to get him to come to some of these meetings. This morning I summoned up my courage and said to him, 'Charlie, I want you to come with me tonight to some meetings we are having down in Wilberforce Hall.' He looked at me and said, 'You don't mean to say you are a Christian?' and I answered, 'Yes, I am.' 'Well,' he said, 'so am I.'"

The man said to me, "Wasn't that funny?"

"Funny!" I said. "No. Is he here? For if so, both you and he need to get down here and start. You never have been born again."

It is an absolute impossibility for two men born again of the Spirit, filled with the Spirit, to work side by side for five years, and neither one nor the other find it out. If one man is a Christian and the other is not, the man that is not will soon see the difference in the work the Christian man does. Christian men do pure, strong work, and the best work in the world.

"But," you say, "I have had a man working for me who doesn't do this, and he is a Christian."

No, he is not! If a man is filled with the spirit of God, it will be manifest in every action of his life; and if you get this capital behind you, it won't be hard work to influence men for Christ; it will be the necessity of your life. The passion of your soul will be to win another soul for Christ, to weave another garland wherewith to deck His brow, to plant another gem in His diadem; and your life will be doing it as well as your words. You must have the capital of God to accomplish the business of God.

And again, that is true about all the activities of life. People often come and ask me questions about amusements: "Should we do this, that, and the other?"

Well, you must only do amusements in which it is possible for the Holy Spirit to reveal Jesus Christ.

You say, "That is very narrow."

No, it isn't, it is very broad. That settles a great many questions of amusements for me. I know young people who make tennis an instrument of the devil. If a man gives himself completely to it, to neglect other things, and to make other people uncomfortable in the world, that is not Christianity. But that, and similar kinds of amusements, can be done as pure recreation, and played so that the very gentleness and beauty of Jesus Christ will be manifested in the playing. Every activity of life, which is in itself right and pure, will shine with glory the moment you become a Spirit-filled soul; and instead of being narrow and shut up within confined walls, you will be able to see that He has set your feet in a large room, He has unlocked for you all avenues of life. Filled with the Spirit, you will be able to manifest the beauty and the glory of the will of God, as against all the rebellion of the age we live in.

And now I want to pose a question to you that you will answer to yourself: How much are you worth?

You know how people usually answer that question. I remember very well in England how we were impressed during one month some years ago by the death of two men, one on this side of the water, and one on that side. The man over here was a millionaire, and the other was Cardinal Manning. As I traveled in a train just about the time these two died, I was impressed by hearing several businessmen talking, and they asked, "Well, how much was he worth?"

"Oh," said one, "so many millions."

"And how much was he worth?" said they of the other.

"Well, he died worth five hundred dollars."

Do you see? We measure things this way; we say a man is worth so much. Don't you see the horror of it now?

What are you worth? I do not ask to know anything about your bank balance. What are you worth? What do you possess?

You say, "I possess so much. I possess my home."

No, no, you do not! What do you possess? You only possess the things you have bought for the kingdom of God. You are rich according to the number of the hours which you have bought up. The time redeemed is wealth. Every time you buy up an opportunity for Him, every time your life reveals itself upon an ungodly man, every time your dealings with God shine out in some of the activities of your life, and every time your sacrifice influences a soul towards God, in that moment of buying up an opportunity, you invest an hour in God, and with those hours God is making your fortune. You are not worth the things you possess upon the earth. They fade and vanish. They are of the earth, earthy. You are only worth the treasure that you have laid at His gates, the influence which you have purchased by sacrifice for Him. These are the things which mark your value and your work and make your fortune.

Oh, what a day it will be when God gives these fortunes back to us! How surprised some will be when the Master comes and says, "You bought up an opportunity one day for Me. You met a soul that was thirsty on the dusty highway of life, and it was an opportunity for you to show that soul what I would have done if I had been there, and you gave that soul a cup of water.

Now here is the result of it," and what it will be, who can say? God will meet you someday, my friend, and He will say, "Do you remember that day in your store when you could have made ten thousand dollars in one stroke, and you didn't because there was a trick and a twist behind it, and you said, 'No, I will be that much poorer for the kingdom of heaven's sake.'" God will say, "That was your investment. See, this is the result," and He will show you how you helped that day to bring in righteousness, and to move with Him towards the consummation of the purposes of His heart of love.

That is how men are making fortunes. Aren't you going in for this kind of business? Aren't you going to start over and say, "I am going to make this life a place in which I accomplish heaven's business. I will take the opportunities as they come and buy them up for God. I will take my home; it is an opportunity which I will purchase for the exhibition of all the beauties of the Christlike character and all the purposes of the divine heart. Life to me from here on will be an opportunity for doing God's business and laying up treasure in heaven."

Is that your determination? Then you must go to the King and say, "O King, I want to be Your businessman on earth. Give me the capital I need. Give me the filling of Your Holy Spirit. Then all my service will be a delight, and I will be able to take all hours, and all activities, and everything that comes to me, and transform them from the dross of earth into the gold of heaven."

May God help every one of us to be His businessmen!

Chapter 8

Gathering or Scattering

We are living in a day that is known as the day of tolerance. We have lost our desire to force our own particular views on other people except by persuasion. Torture and excommunication are things of the past. And I believe that there cannot be too much toleration. No one has any right to take the judgment throne of Jesus Christ and pass sentence upon his fellow citizens. But while this is perfectly true, we cannot forget that the very freedom of the atmosphere in which we live has produced in individual life an indifference to the truth of God. As much as we belittle any attempt by persecution to compel belief, we cannot close our eyes to the fact that the old days of persecution were also the days of purity in the church of Christ. It is very remarkable that the church of Christ persecuted has been the church of Christ pure. The church of Christ patronized has always become the church of Christ impure.

The very saddest day in church history was the day that Constantine embraced the cause of Christianity. When an earthly emperor and empire took upon themselves to patronize the Nazarene, and to say that the religion of the Nazarene should have a position under the wing of the state, that day there passed into Christendom the most damning and blemishing influence that has ever touched it. Men and women, when they had to face death for the things that they held to, were pure. Men and women who were not prepared to do this kept themselves outside the churches of Jesus Christ. All that has passed away. No one will persecute you now for being a Christian. There is a sense, I know, in which *all who desire to live godly in Christ Jesus will be persecuted* (2 Timothy 3:12), but the old days of fiery tests of faith have passed away. With their passing we have entered a region of peril. The peril that threatens us today is that of indifference.

Now, if this is true – and you know it is – it is well for us sometimes to come into the presence of Jesus Christ and learn that while no man has any right to pronounce sentence upon us, Christ has that right. And not only does He have the right to do that, but in unmistakable language in His teaching He has also made a clean line of demarcation between man and man, setting certain people on one side and certain people on the other. No verse that I know of in the whole realm of the teaching of Jesus Christ is more searching than Matthew 12:30: *"He who is not with Me is against Me; and he who does not gather with Me scatters."*

One can imagine that it fell from the lips of Jesus quietly and calmly, but it is a true throne of judgment, dividing men swiftly and surely into two opposite camps, leaving no *via media,* no middle way, no neutral ground. As the Master said these words in the old days, and by uttering them divided the crowd in front of Him, from that time until now, through every successive century, amongst all sorts and conditions of people, this verse has come as the line of divine division, separating people to the right and to the left.

People from many different circumstances are here in this gathering, but as God looks upon us, He moves us to the right and to the left. He ranks us among the gatherers or the scatterers. No one takes a middle position.

A great and terrible mistake we are constantly making today is that of comparing ourselves with ourselves. We test the experience of today with the experience of yesterday. We allow ourselves to be puffed up because we think that our conduct is a little superior to everyone else's. Now, let's stop all this comparison of self with self and person with person. Let's come to the judgment seat of Jesus Christ and see what He means and where we stand in the light of it.

In order that we may rightly do that, we must first understand what our Lord meant when He said, *"He who is not with Me is against Me; and he who does not gather with Me scatters."* I will, therefore, first consider briefly the claim that Jesus Christ makes for Himself. Inferentially, and yet with perfect clearness, He sets up on His own behalf a certain very definite claim. Secondly, we will see how that claim defines our position.

What is the claim that the Master sets up for Himself? Listen: *"He who is not with Me is against Me."* So far, we have no claim made; but in order that the statement may be understood, He goes on to explain it by saying, *"He who does not gather with Me scatters."* His claim is that He is the Gatherer. His mission to the world was to gather together.

Having set up this claim for Himself, He proceeds to say to the men and women around Him, that every human being is exercising through life the great force that gathers together with Christ, or that other force, which is of hell, that scatters abroad against Christ. Christ claims for Himself that He is God's Gatherer. Christ says that every man is either with Him or against Him, gathering or scattering.

Let us take these two things and look at them a little more closely, patiently, and prayerfully, so that we can understand them. What does the Master mean when He says *gather with*

Me? In John 11:49 and following is a passage that throws light on the subject: *But one of them, Caiaphas, who was high priest that year, said to them, "You know nothing at all, nor do you take into account that it is expedient for you that one man die for the people, and that the whole nation not perish instead."*

I am not interested for the moment in these extraordinary words that Caiaphas uttered, but I move on to what comes after that, and which is an inspired exposition of the priest's words: *Now he did not say this on his own initiative, but being high priest that year, he prophesied that Jesus was going to die for the nation, and not for the nation only, but in order that He might also gather together into one the children of God who are scattered abroad* (John 11:51-52). It is thus most explicitly stated that *not for the nation only*, but *the children of God who are scattered abroad* are to be gathered. Jesus Christ came into the world to gather into one the scattered family of the Most High.

Now, put aside this Gospel narrative and consider the day in which we live. There is a phrase that has been on the lips and pens of certain men a lot for the last twenty-five years or more: "the solidarity of humanity." It is one of those phrases that sounds as if there were a good deal in it, and men have made the most of it. They have written books under the impulse of what is behind that phrase; they have formulated philosophies, designing them on that phrase.

Trench tells us that it comes to us from the Communists. The solidarity of humanity. What do they mean when they talk about the solidarity of humanity? It means that humanity is not a gathering together of units, each one separate and alone, but that humanity is one; that all men are dependent upon all other men, and that the race is united from its beginning to its end; that this particular generation of which you and I are a part owes an enormous amount to the generations that have preceded it; that we are helping make the history of the generations that will come after us; that what Kingsley sang about the newborn baby is perfectly true – that that child is "heir of all the ages."

Not only is humanity one when you trace it in its movements through history, but it is also one in its relationship today. Every nation of the world is linked to every other nation of the world. We owe something to other men; other men owe much to us. "No man lives unto himself." The race is one, bound up by bonds that cannot be broken.

Now, if Trench is right, that we get that phrase from the Communists, then we do not get the truth that is enshrined in it from the Communists because it is a divine truth. It is a revelation of the purpose and thought of God for humanity.

What is God's thought for the human race? Hear it in these words of inspiration: *"He made from one man every nation of mankind to live on all the face of the earth"* (Acts 17:26). The divine ideal for humanity is that humanity is to be one family; that man should serve his brother man, and in that service find his purest delight; that man should make perpetual acknowledgment every day and always of his indebtedness to his fellow man; that there should be no self-consciousness and self-seeking which is at the expense of the right and the comfort and the blessedness of other men. That is the divine ideal. It is upon that ideal of humanity that Jesus Christ based all His work and all His teaching, and upon which the apostles of Jesus Christ accomplished their mission in the world.

But is this realized? As I said, men are writing about it. America has produced some men who have dreamed wonderful dreams along this very line. A most remarkable man, Edward Bellamy, recently died, whose books I have read with keen interest and have detected beneath them the aspiration of a great heart after a divine ideal that he never understood; and the trouble is, Edward Bellamy wanted to get society into the kingdom of God without taking it by way of the cross of Jesus Christ, and he could never do it. He and other dreamers of beautiful dreams, in which men will lose the miserable idea that any work is dishonorable, wanted to pass into that realm outside the actual, positive, interfering government of God, but it can never be done. You cannot grow the tulips of the kingdom of God unless you get the bulbs from heaven. Never forget that.

The fact is, that is an ideal, a dream. How about the realization? There is a great disintegration of humanity. We are broken up; we are split; we are divided. Look where you will, and you see that the divine ideal of the human race is lost. I do not want to be misunderstood at this point, but I feel that you are ready to take a high and spiritual outlook upon these things, and that you will bear with me patiently when I say that nationality is a poor business; that patriotism is something that perhaps is necessary for today, in the midst of the chaos and breakup of the great ideal of God for humanity; but that in the day when the King shall reign, we will not talk anymore about my nationality versus yours.

We will enter into the larger ideal that we are one, the world over; that every man with the image of God upon him, and the breath of God in him, is a brother man, to be loved, served, and cared for. We will move away from the idea that because we are a great and mighty nation we have any right to override and destroy other nations that are weaker than we are. We will learn that every man has rights because he is a child of God, and we will respect them. But that time has not come yet. If you want to know something about the disintegration of humanity versus the solidarity of humanity, see the civilized, the Christianized (God forgive us for abusing that word!) nations of Europe watching each other with a suspicion that is devilish and horrible. There is nothing of the spirit of Christ in it.

Come down from the national outlook and consider the

home. There is nothing that is saddening me more in England today than the breakup of our homelife; that the old family circles that made a poet write these words: "The heart has many a dwelling place, but only once a home," are passing away from our country. Children are growing away from their parents, and parents from their children, and the old strong bands that made up a strong nation because we were strong in our family relationships are being broken. Everywhere there are marks of disintegration.

Then look at the church of God. Do you get any comfort out of the division in the church of God? I hope you do not. I hope you have never said that it is part of the divine plan that Christendom should be split into a thousand fragments. I tell you it is not. He who prayed the great intercessory prayer which took hold of heaven in my behalf and your behalf for all time, said, "Father, I will *that they may all be one; . . . so that the world may believe that You sent Me*" (John 17:21). We are not one, and that is why the world doesn't know that God sent Jesus.

Look at the details of life, and you will find the same breakup everywhere; instead of there being oneness in the human family, there is infinite division and infinite distrust. Men do not trust each other in business or in social life or in church life. Everywhere there are the marks of a great disintegrating force which has broken humanity into a thousand parts, and the great ideal of the oneness of the race is lost.

Christ came to gather into one the children of God who are scattered. That was His mission. How is He going to do it? He will do it, as God does everything, fundamentally. He will never tinker with externals; He will go to the heart of the matter. He will never attempt to paint on the outside that which is rotten. He will demolish that which is old, and He will bring in better things. And how does He do it? He comes into the midst of men Himself to reveal God, to restore the divine government, to do battle in His own life and in His cross and passion, with the sin that has divided humanity.

That was His mission. He came to gather. He came to wipe out the lines that create nationalities and to bring us back into the one family of God; to bind together into closer harmony the families of the earth; to heal the breach between man and man; to drive away from the earth every form of difference and dissension.

But someone says, "Didn't He say, 'I am come to send a sword'?"

That was a statement of the necessity of the gospel He preached. He knew the condition of man, and He knew that His announcement of divine kingship, the only truth that could ever heal the divisions, must, before the great work is completed, scatter the sword, and apparently tear humanity further and further apart. But that tearing is only that which precedes the healing, and the sword He sends is the sword which makes way for purity and opens the door for peace. So, He came to gather.

Oh, how one would like to take up His life and look at it in that light! His teachings, His miracles, look at Him again! Healing wounds, gathering a few men together in the first place, and saying to them, *"Who is My mother and who are My brothers? For whoever does the will of My Father . . . is My brother and sister and mother"* (Matthew 12:48, 50). What did He mean? He meant to say, "Here is the higher relationship, above the relationship of blood, the relationship of spiritual affinity in the kingdom of God; and mother and brothers pass out of sight in the presence of this new relationship." He says to me, as He said to the people then, "If you are going to follow Me, you must leave your father, mother, and husband and wife. You must put Me first."

I say, "Master, that is a hard thing to do."

He replies, "But that is what I did for you. I put you before

My mother and brothers. If you come to Me, you must do as much for Me as I have done for you."

And so He created that little spiritual circle, and He came to gather others into it, and thank God, His work will never cease until He Himself comes again and establishes the kingdom out of which He will drive all dissension, and into which He will gather the children of God that are scattered abroad. It is the great work of Christ to heal the wounds, to make dissension cease, and to bring the world around Himself into a sacred brotherhood, in the fatherhood of God. That is the great mission of Christ.

Now I come to the second point. After that vision of His work, what does He say? *"He who is not with Me is against Me; and he who does not gather with Me scatters."*

Jesus came to gather, and He says that I am helping or hindering, with Him or against Him; that I am gathering or scattering. Let me say, first, that the influence I exert in the world is created by my relationship to Jesus Christ. If I am with Him, I am a gatherer. If I am His and He is mine, if Christ is actually in me, what will be the effect? I will be gathering with Him, bringing men to Him; and in bringing men to Him I am bringing men to each other. Did that ever occur to you?

The Man stands amid humanity and is its center of attraction Godward and heavenward. In proportion that men are brought near to Him, in that proportion they are coming near to each other; and any attempt to get men near together, apart from the attraction of Jesus Christ and His power to hold them together, is a dream that cannot be realized. Men have the dream of unity, but they have not seen the center of attraction to unite them.

And how will it happen? It will begin in your home. You will gather your children together first. It has been a long time since Christians ceased trying to gather men together who live in the slums and gave their time to getting their children together. One of my deacons once said to me casually, lightly, smilingly, as though it were a very pretty, pleasing thing to say, "Do you know, Mr. Morgan, I don't see my *bairns* ("children"; he had two beautiful children). I haven't seen my *bairns* awake for several months."

I said to him, "What do you mean?"

"Well," he said, "don't you see, I have been so fearfully busy; business is growing at such a rate that I am up and off in the morning before they are awake, and I do not get home at night until after they are in bed; and on Sunday I am down at the church all day, and I hardly see them then."

I said to him, "My dear brother, for God's sake and for your children's sake, drop something in your business; and if you cannot do that, drop something at the church, and look after your *bairns.* It is an infinitely better investment to give your time to them and to keep your hand on them than anything else you can do."

A man that cannot hold his family together for Christ by the attractive power of Christ in his own life is not wanted in the church; keep him out. That man cannot do anything for God in public places if his own home is devastated and broken up by the principle of rebellion against God. And if the influence a man is exerting on his family is an influence that scatters, that man is not with Christ. If you are with Christ, hold your *bairns* for Him, and your family will be God's first circle of the kingdom, as it always has been, and it will be a witness to the power of Christ in you, and through you, to gather men together.

We had a sensation across the ocean a few years ago, an artistic sensation. Men raved about dandelions and lilies. Men posed in womanly postures and said that they could exist for a week upon a lily. It was neurotic; it was rotten; and the high priest of the whole business, the apostle of the artistic sensation, had to go to prison as a common prisoner for beastliness of conduct that cannot be named in public. If you try to gather men together by painting a lily on a plate and giving them a sweet willow pattern – oh God, the mockery of it! You cannot touch men's hearts like that. If you are not with Christ, you cannot gather men.

I don't care what your philosophy is, what your policy is, or what the basis of art is, or education, or culture, or anything you please. No power the world has ever heard, taught, or preached, except the power of the crucified, risen Christ, is sufficient to gather men together into one.

You say, "Can't we improve the dwellings of the poor?"

Yes, God help us to do it; but one of the best ways to do it is to improve the man that lives in the dwelling.

I remember some years ago conducting a mission, and one of the office-bearers of the church where I was said to me, "Mr. Morgan, I want you to come and see some people. Three years ago, a girl in our Sunday school married a man who was a slave to drink and impurity and gambling. I would like you to come with me and see her."

I went – it was in 1885 – on a cold February day to see that girl. Oh, I cannot describe the home to you! It was one of those awful houses in the Midlands of England, reached by passing through an entry between other houses, into a back court. When I got to the entry with my friend, some children who were hovering and shivering there, hearing our steps approaching, ran away. We followed them and went into the house. I can see that room now. There was a broken table standing there, a chair with the back broken off standing by it, no fire in the fireplace; on the mantel was a broken cup and saucer; and there was not another article of furniture that I could see in the room. And there stood a woman in unwomanly rags with the bruise of a brutal fist on her face, and three ill-clad children clinging to her dress. She said, "Excuse the children running from you, but they thought that it was Father."

Oh, the tragedy of it!

When I got onto the platform that night to preach, my friend came to me and said, "He is here."

I said, "Who is here?"

"That woman's husband; he is sitting right down in front of you."

Now, I do not often preach to one man, but I did that night. I put aside what I was going to talk about, and read the story of the Prodigal Son, and I asked God to help me talk about it; and for about a solid hour I preached to that man. Do you think I hammered at him and scolded him? No. I told him God loved him, there and then; and when we got to the invitation, I asked, "What man is coming home tonight?" He was the very first to rise. He came forward, and as I went down from the platform and gave that meeting into someone else's hands, I got my arm around him and prayed and wept with him. He entered into the kingdom of God.

My friend said to me one day about twelve months later, "I want you to go and see some people."

I said, "Who?"

He said, "Do you remember going to see a woman last year whose husband was converted? I want you to come and see those people."

I went. We had not gone far – it was February of the next year – before I said to him, "Friend, where are you taking me?"

"Oh, we are going to see those people."

"But," I said, "we are not going the same way."

"No," he said, "they have moved."

Moved! Why did they move? Why, the man was converted, and he soon changed where he lived. The man was remade, and he remade his environment; and he had gone, not into a palace, but into a cottage in the main street.

If I could paint pictures, I would paint those two. I can see that home now. It was on a Sunday, after the afternoon service, and he sat by the fire with his three children, who had run away from him a year ago. One was on his knee, another on his shoulder, and another stood by him; and I never heard a sweeter solo in my life than the solo the kettle sang on the fireplace shelf that day. The woman that was dressed in unwomanly rags last year was clothed, and the sunlight of love was on her face.

That is how you must deal with the problem of environment. Begin at its middle. Touch the man who makes the beastly environment, remake him, and he will soon move out of the tenement house and out of the slum. He will soon find his way onto higher levels. That is the way to gather men and women. Unless you are with Jesus Christ, you can try education and culture, but it all comes short of life, and without life there is no remaking of men.

Now, my friend, are you with Christ in this enterprise?

My last word is a reversal of that position. And now we come to this text as to a judgment seat. It is not only true that your influence will be created by your relationship to Jesus Christ; it is also true that your relationship to Jesus Christ will be revealed by the influence you are exercising.

I am getting less and less anxious to hear what men say. What is the influence you are exerting in the world? Show me a man who is gathering men, who is healing wounds, who is closing up breaches, who is coming into life with a sacred, subtle, forceful manner which makes men love each other because he is there; that man is with Christ. I am not particular as to whether he spells his denomination with a *P* or a *C,* or anything you like; the point is whether he is gathering men. May God help us to stop trying to order men out of service because they do not follow with us.

You say, "You know it is apostolic."

I am not particular about being in apostolic succession; they have made such miserable blunders. Go to the Gospel of Mark chapter 9. John said unto Christ, *"Teacher, we saw someone casting out demons."*

"Oh, did you? You must have been glad, John."

"Yes, and it was done in Your name."

"Blessed work! Glorious work! I want to know that man."

"Then we saw someone casting out devils in Your name, and we stopped him."

"Why, why?"

"Because he did not follow us." *"Not following us,"* it really says. *"Because he was not following us."*

But Jesus said, "Do not hinder him, for there is no one who will perform a miracle in My name, and be able soon afterward to speak evil of Me. For he who is not against us is for us."

Ah, that is the test! Do you know a man that casts out devils, my dear friend, in the Presbyterian church, and he isn't a Presbyterian? Do not hinder him. "Oh no," you say, "we wouldn't think of doing that; he is a Congregationalist." But suppose he isn't that; suppose he is none of your *-ists* and your *-isms;* suppose he is just a man that has gotten in touch with Christ and hardly knows the truth himself yet. Leave him alone! He cannot work a work in the name of Christ and speak evil of Him. If he is not against Christ, he is with Him. Take this larger outlook, this practical test of position.

But there is another word which is part of that last thought: A man who scatters is not a Christian.

Do you know that man who has lost his children?

"What do you mean? A man that has buried them?"

Oh no, no! God help him, it would have been better if he

had, long ago. He has *lost* them. He has no hold on them, no influence over them. They have gone from his home and scattered, and leaving his house they have gone from his God with great relief. They were glad to go away from him to get away from his God, and they are swearing against God today.

"Why?"

Because of that man's influence.

"But that man is a church member."

I do not care; he is not a Christian.

"But that man preaches."

I do not care; if he has lost his children it is because he has not been with Christ, but has been against Him. Show me the man that is splitting and dividing the church, dividing the nation, and setting man against man; that man is not a Christian. I do not care what his subscription is, what his profession is, what noise he makes in the world; all these things are nothing. If that man is not gathering with Jesus, he is scattering; and if he is scattering, he is not *with* Christ, he is *against* Christ.

So much for the teaching of that verse, as I understand it. Now, where are you, and where am I? Am I with the Master, or am I against Him?

You say, "Well, I am not exactly with Him, but I am not against Him."

You are wrong. There is no middle place.

"Oh," you say, "there must be a middle place. I have never done anything for Him; I have never led a soul to Him; I have never preached for Him or spoken for Him, or given a tract away for Him, or even given a cup of cold water for His sake; but I have never hindered Him; I haven't spoken against Him; I haven't denounced Christianity."

Some of you have been in London. When you visit London again, get down in the center of the great city and stand still and look in a window. You will not be there long before a man in blue will put his hand on your shoulder and say, "Please move on."

"Why should I move on?"

"You are blocking the traffic."

"I am not interfering with anyone."

"Your standing still and doing nothing is going to cause an obstruction here; you must please move on. Keep moving. You can go this way, or you can go that way, but you cannot stand still; you must move."

My brother, my sister, you cannot stand still. The moment you stand still and say, "I am just going to be an interested onlooker," you become an obstacle in His way, you slow His progress. If you stand, someone else is going to stand. Don't you know that? You cannot stand still without impeding progress. If you are not with Him, you are against Him. If you are not exercising the great force that gathers, by your very negation of that, you are exercising the force that scatters men here and there and everywhere.

Men and women, will you take sides? Stop trying to be neutral, I ask you. Whether you have ever professed to be a Christian or not, I do not care. I appeal to you now. I call for men and women to take sides definitely and positively in this matter. The great Lord Jesus, sweet and strong, tender and mighty, came from heaven to earth to gather men together, and He says everyone is either helping Him or hindering Him. Which is it?

Do not say, I ask you, "It is no use for me to pretend to take sides with Christ; I can do so little."

It is your life that helps Him, not the extra activity in which you engage now and again. What the Master wants today in all the cities and villages of England and America is men and women who are living with Him. America is waiting for the manifestation of the sons and daughters of God, and wherever you are manifested to be related to God in Christ, you become part of the great force that is gathering men together. You contribute by that relationship to God in Christ to the work of Christ in healing wounds, closing up the breaches, and making all the families of the earth one, as God has determined they should be.

What we want is not to ask men so much to take sides, because they are doing that whether or not; what we need is to appeal to them to take the side of Christ. Isn't it better to construct than to destroy, to heal than to wound, to gather men than to scatter them? Then will you not be among the number of those who come to the Nazarene and say, "Oh, Jesus, by Your infinite compassion, by Your love surpassing all human strength, You have conquered me. I come to You. Take my life, poor, weak, insufficient by every standard of human measurement, but let Your life flow into it, and through it, that my life may make some little contribution to the realization of Your great purpose."

Lord Jesus, from today let me more than ever be a gatherer of Yours. Prevent me from scattering. Do this, Lord, by taking complete possession of me more than ever before. To this end I yield to You all that I am, and have, and hope for, in order that through me some part of Your kingdom may come and Your will be done. Amen.

Chapter 9

The Danger of Pitching
Your Tent toward Sodom

Lot . . . moved his tents as far as Sodom.
(Genesis 13:12)

While a great many details in the story of Lot are purely local, and their color has faded, the underlying principles are full of meaning and application for today. And so I propose to ask you to look with me at this man Lot. Lot was a good man who acted upon a wrong principle with disastrous results. Now, it may be almost a startling thing to say that Lot was a good man. I am bound to confess that if I only had the story of the history that I find in the Old Testament, I would hardly have come to that conclusion, but my failure to understand Lot would have been due to my inability to read the story correctly. In the New Testament it is distinctly declared that he was a *righteous man* (2 Peter 2:8).

I repeat, therefore, that this is the story of a good man – good, that is, in intention, good in the deepest desire of his heart, perfectly sincere in many ways, and always desiring to be right; and yet becoming so sadly wrong that today he stands out on the page of Holy Scripture not as an example of one in whose steps we should follow, but as a warning, in order that we may avoid his pathway. What a strange contradiction this is – a good man held up as a warning, a man who meant well, and yet so lived that the one thing we need to be careful of in life is that we do not live as he lived.

Is it not true that there are thousands of such people in the world today? I am not at all sure that if it were possible for us to analyze the inner life of the great majority of people, we would not find them in very much the same condition. They mean well, and think that they would always choose the good and refuse the evil; and yet they are very often doing evil and refusing the good. They seem to be strange contradictions – men who want to be right, and are wrong; men who admire the things that are high and noble and beautiful, and yet do the things that are low and mean and despicable.

Lot was such a man, and therefore it must be of great interest, I think, that we should attempt to discover his mistake, to trace it to its completion, so that we may be warned from following in his footsteps.

Now, first, let me remind you that this man Lot had been closely associated with Abram from his first move, from his move with Terah from Ur of the Chaldees. Let us go back and read one or two verses, to give us the sequence of the history. In Genesis 11:31 I read: *Terah took Abram his son, and Lot the son of Haran, his grandson, and Sarai his daughter-in-law, his son Abram's wife;* – will you notice what happened – *and they went out together from Ur of the Chaldeans in order to enter the land of Canaan;* – but they did not get to Canaan – *and they went as far as Haran, and settled there.* That was the first move, and it would almost seem as though originally the move was not that of Abram, but that of his father, Terah. What I want you especially to notice, however, is that Lot was with them.

Now go to Genesis 12:5. *Abram took Sarai his wife and Lot his nephew, and all their possessions which they had accumulated, and the persons which they had acquired in Haran, and they set out for the land of Canaan; thus they came to the land of Canaan.* That was the second move. They waited in Haran until Terah died, and then they moved on again, again heading for the land of Canaan, and this time arriving there. Notice especially that Lot was still with them.

Now in Genesis 13:1 I read: *So Abram went up from Egypt to the Negev, he and his wife and all that belonged to him, and Lot with him.* So you see that Lot had been with Abram when he went down into Egypt – something Abram should never have done – and after that Abram came up out of Egypt and Lot was still with him. Now we come to that crisis in the lives of the two men when they parted from each other. It is in this connection that the true character, both of Abram and Lot, is revealed before us.

Notice the crisis for a moment. Domestic difficulties had arisen which had in them elements of discord. Abram and Lot had become very wealthy. The herdsmen of the two men quarreled over pasture for the flocks. Abram, with the magnanimity of a great soul and the foresight of a great statesman, said to Lot, *"Please let there be no strife between you and me, nor between my herdsmen and your herdsmen, for we are brothers. Is not the whole land before you? Please separate from me; if to the left, then I will go to the right; or if to the right, then I will go to the left."*

It is under these circumstances that the true character of Lot is manifested. He lifted up his eyes, and he saw the well-watered plain of the Jordan; and he saw down there on the plain the cities in which the men of the plain had congregated and were living for commercial pursuits and making money. He chose to move in that direction; and in that choice, we have a revelation of the man. Parting company from Abram, he *pitched his tent,* as the King James Version has it, *toward Sodom.*

Now, these are small matters. First, it was a very small matter that created the crisis which manifested the character of Abram and Lot. The choosing of this particular place was a small matter. The crises that test men are always small. A man is never revealed when he is prepared for the occasion of examination. We are never really manifested if we have been notified beforehand that we are going to be examined. Scholastic examinations are really no test of what a man knows.

It is true in every area of life, that the test announced and prepared for, sometimes by cramming, is often at fault, when we want to know what a man is or knows. God never announces His examinations. If God were to announce to us tonight that tomorrow at twelve o'clock He would meet us in order to find out what we were in character, what preparations there would be between now and twelve o'clock tomorrow. How careful we would be to appear at our very best, and the result would be false. What you are shows when you do not know anyone is likely to be watching you critically.

In the small things, in the little details, in the commonplaceness of life, character shines out. I never try to find out what a preacher is when he is preaching. It is when he is home and when he thinks there is no one there to critically watch him, that that is the time to find out what he is really like. I never want to find out what a deacon is like in a deacons' meeting. Sometimes you do, but that is not the best time. The time to find that out is on Monday, Tuesday, Wednesday, during the week. I do not want to know what your character is when you are singing. I want to find out what your character is when something goes wrong, some little commonplace problem with your work at home. When you are carried along by the stream of the commonplace, then your character is revealed.

The characters of these two men are revealed forevermore, when their servants begin quarreling. The herdsmen of Abram and the herdsmen of Lot, to use an everyday expression, are just having a quarrel, and on the basis of that quarrel between the herdsmen, the character of Abram is revealed and the character of Lot is revealed. I know what Lot is and what Abram is in the light of that very unpleasant and absurdly ridiculous quarrel between men whom they employed and paid.

Many people have been revealed in their true light over quarrels with other people about mere trifles. It was Charles Haddon Spurgeon, that prince of preachers, who once said, "I will find out what pattern your creed is, not when I look at you in the sanctuary, but as I see you on Sunday morning, getting ready for church, if certain things are not to your hand as you think they ought to be." It was a quaint, forceful, illuminative statement of a great truth about character. I see Lot, I see Abram, and I see the inner, underlying principle of life in the case of each, and all the subsequent history is true to the revelation of character that flashes out when their herdsmen are quarreling.

Let us look at Lot. When I finish I will ask you to look at Abram by way of contrast. But our focus now is on Lot. First, we will look at his choice; second, we will look at the results that follow his choice; and then we will conclude by attempting to draw the very evident lessons from the study that we can profit from as we live our lives.

First, we ask, Was it wrong to choose? Certainly not. The supreme dignity of human life is that it is made to choose. The greatest gift that you possess is the gift of will – the fact that there comes to you every day, every hour, and I think I can safely say every moment, something concerning which you have to elect, to decide, to choose. We are not automatic machines.

We are independent, free agents. I can choose heaven or hell. It is a tremendous issue, but it is a magnificent possibility. That is the dignity of human life. If we were but machines, then the romance, the poetry, and the passion of life would be at an end. If I must, then I must, and the colors fade from the sky, and everything becomes ashen and gray. It lacks iron, force, vigor, and virtue. Life is life to me because I must choose. There are often moments when we would almost wish that someone else could choose for us, and in our childhood days, though a passion for choice arose, it was a gracious thing that others had to choose for us. But it would be a sad thing if we always remained children.

In the very possession of our being is the right to choose, this capacity for decision, this magnificent power that God allows us. In life every man must choose. Lot made his choice. What, then, was wrong? Carefully notice the principle of his choice, and the purpose of his choice, as we have them revealed in the actual words of Scripture. I do not want to depart in imagination from Scripture, but will read Genesis 13:11: *So Lot chose for himself all the valley of the Jordan, and Lot journeyed eastward. Thus they separated from each other.* Now go back a verse: *Lot lifted up his eyes and saw all the valley of the Jordan,* and when he looked, what did he see? He saw *that it was well watered everywhere . . . like the garden of the Lord, like the land of Egypt as you go to Zoar.*

First you have the purpose of his choice revealed in that very little sentence that we read so carelessly – *Lot chose for himself.* The central purpose of his choice was that of selfishness – Lot chose for *himself.* A moment has come in the life of the man when it is necessary for him to choose. He must make a choice, and he proceeds to exercise his will upon the basis of personal desire alone. He *chose for himself,* he chose something for himself, something that would minister to himself. He put outside the realm of the things that moved him everything except his own desire, and his own desire in these things was that which would minister to his own self-life. There is a revealing sentence here: *Lot chose for himself all the valley of the Jordan.* He was already a wealthy man. He had gotten great gain while living with Abram, but he is still seeking gain, and self is the underlying reason.

We see now what the principle was. You may say it was not wrong to get gain. He was already a wealthy man; they were both wealthy. There was surely nothing wrong in gain. Notice here carefully, however, that desiring simply for himself, he is entering upon a compromise between two wrong principles. Again, two little sentences manifest this. He sees all the wonderful *valley of the Jordan.* Notice what two things attracted him – *like the garden of the Lord, like the land of Egypt.*

Ah, yes, this man has recently been down to Egypt. He has seen its commerce, he has seen its wealth, he has seen its sordidness, he has seen its blinded materialism, and he wants to be able to get gain as the Egyptians are getting gain. He has seen that down in those cities of Egypt gain was gotten faster than it ever could be when living a nomadic life. Here is a quicker way to live and get gain, to live in nearness to a city. *Like the land of Egypt,* and yet *like the garden of the Lord.*

What Lot is attempting to do is to bring two things together which are in opposition to each other. It is the principle of compromise, and when he makes his choice, he does not go straight into Sodom and live there; he *moved his tents as far as Sodom,* and lived near it. You see without multiplication of words what this man is doing. He says in his heart, "Now my chance has come. I have been with Abram a long time, I have believed in his God and in his faith, but he is a little behind the times, he is a little old-fashioned, he is just a tiny bit fanatical. I cannot get him away from the tent and the altar. Wherever he goes, he pitches a tent and builds an altar; and again he moves the tent and the altar. He is always wandering; he is not settled. So I will move my tent toward Sodom; I will get as near to it as I can. Sodom is wicked. I have no desire to share its wickedness. I am not drawn toward its evil, but I will be near enough to it to get gain out of it."

The day Lot moved his tent as far as Sodom, there was, first, a selfish motive behind his choice: *Lot chose for himself*; and there was, moreover, the fact that he tried to compromise: he got his good, and yet got near enough to evil to gain something out of it. I am not at all sure, indeed I am personally inclined to believe, that when he moved his tent toward Sodom he hoped not merely to get something out of it, but to also put something into it. "I may do these people good, I may influence them along my line of life, I may be able to help them, I may be able to use the purity of a simple faith, I may be able to do something to bring them near the true and living God. I am going there to make wealth faster than I can in the old-fashioned way. Abram's God I worship and I love, but I will choose for myself, and I will endeavor to make a compromise to get as near to Sodom as I can in order that I may have the advantage of life *like the garden of the Lord,* and that of the city where wealth may be made faster than it can be by men in tents moving from place to place." It was a choice based upon purely personal and selfish reasoning.

In the light of things seen, Lot for the moment had shut out of his vision the unseen things. He was acting as though this life was everything, as though the only thing worth thinking about was wealth, as though the supreme aim of existence was that of becoming increasingly wealthy. The man's eyes are fastened upon the earth, and he does not see the gleaming light of the spiritual realm. He has forgotten the things that are permanent and is attempting to grasp the things that are perishing. *Lot chose for himself,* and it was a choice that was selfish and compromising.

But how did this work out? What followed? What was the sequel? I again want to read verses that are remarkable in revealing the sequel, and easily remembered. Read this text in chapter 13 first: *[He] moved his tents as far as Sodom.* Carefully notice that he moved not into the city, but near it – just near enough to be able to use it. Turn to chapter 14 and you will find something else. In Genesis 14:12 read these words: *They also took Lot, Abram's nephew, and his possessions and departed, for he was living in Sodom.*

Now, how much time elapsed between these two verses I cannot tell you, but certainly not very much. When he left Abram, he did not go into Sodom, he went near it; but in the very next chapter I find that he has moved into Sodom. It is a natural sequence. He went near Sodom to make use of it. He was near enough to reap some of its advantages, but it would be so much more convenient if he went into it. Now I find him no longer living in a tent, but in a house; no longer near Sodom, but in the midst of it; no longer separated from Sodom, but mixed up in its life.

Move on and see how this ends. I go to Genesis 19:1 and I read these words: *Now the two angels came to Sodom in the evening as Lot was sitting at the gate of Sodom.* We read that, and it does not mean to us necessarily and immediately what it ought to mean. *Sitting at the gate* is a peculiarly Eastern phrase, which brings up a picture of Eastern life. It simply means that he had become the chief magistrate in the city. The chief magistrate of these Eastern cities sat at the gate to decide questions of dispute between the inhabitants, and to receive visitors as the representative of the city's hospitality.

If you will let me translate that little phrase, *Lot was sitting in the gate of Sodom,* into the language of today, into more familiar phraseology, it is exactly as though it were stated that Lot had become the mayor of Sodom. There had been great advancement. First, he raised his tent toward Sodom, then he dwelt in Sodom, and now he is the mayor of Sodom.

It appears as though he is getting on wonderfully well. He is a great success. If that man lived today, his biography would be sold and given away to young men as an example of how to succeed in the world. Oh, this gospel of getting on! I wish I could get rid of it forever. I can almost suggest a title for the book: *From the Tent to the Mayor's Chair; or, How to Succeed in Life.* I pick up a book and I read, *From Log Cabin to White House.* I am not going to cast any shadow on Garfield, but I do say that his greatness was not proved by the fact that he left the log cabin and reached the White House. He was a great man in the cabin. If a man succeeds and gets into a position, becomes mayor or president, and thinks that is everything, it is a lie, and the sooner those facing life get rid of such an idea, the better.

I wonder where Abram is. He is still there in that old tent by the oaks of Mamre; he has made no progress. He is still pitching his tent and building his altar; he is far behind the times. It is Lot who has gotten on.

But now I want to talk to Lot for a little while. I want to ask him a few questions. I want to put him into the witness-box, and I want you to hear his evidence. Lot, you have made a great success of this. You have pitched your tent toward Sodom, and finding that not to be so convenient as it would be to be *in* Sodom, you went in, and you must have gotten on wonderfully well if they made you mayor, and made you to sit in the gate.

But I want to ask you four things, Lot. How has this move affected your own inner life? How has this move affected your own mind? How has this move affected your own heart? And then I want to ask you, How has this move affected your family, whom you took into Sodom with you? And then I want to know how your coming into Sodom affected Sodom. And then I want to ask the meanest thing – and I put it last, though it might have been asked first – How much money did you make by the time you were done? If you want to get on in life, surely these questions are fair. How will your move act upon your heart and conscience, your loved ones, upon the city into which you went, and lastly, how much money will you make from the transaction?

Let us begin with the first. Lot, how about yourself? You are mayor of the city, how about your own heart and mind? Looking at the New Testament I have the answer. Listen. Lot was distressed by the lascivious life of the wicked (*for . . . that righteous man, while living among them, felt his righteous soul tormented day after day by their lawless deeds* (2 Peter 2:8)).

That is the picture of discontent! Surely when the man got on this way, he must have been content. No, discontented! Surely when a man moved into the city, and lived among them, and became mayor, he had peace. No, he vexed his soul, his heart was hot and restless. He had seen the vision of the higher things, and therefore he was never satisfied with the lower. If you want to know where rest is, and peace is, and quietness is, and joy is, it is with old-fashioned Abram up there in the tent, under the oaks, the man who never chose upon the basis of the desire of selfishness, but always upon the basis of the divine will and government; and the man who always lived not merely seeing the things perishing, but also the eternal things, the infinite and undying things.

Lot lost his peace and rest when he went into Sodom. If you have lost your own heart's ease, there is nothing that can make up for it. You may make your fortune, you may gain your position, you may make money, but if your heart is hot and restless, you will make a disastrous failure of it.

An old woman living way up on the wild north coast of my

country, when Christmas Day arrived, she had absolutely nothing for her Christmas dinner upon her table except a piece of bread and a glass of water. And a Christian person who, thinking of the old lady on that glad day, went to her about midday to take her something, and found her already sitting down to her Christmas dinner, which consisted of the bread and the water. She was very hard of hearing and did not hear the footsteps of the person who came into her little cottage. This person heard the old woman ask God's blessing. With eyes shut, and hands clasped, and that sweet, indescribable light on her face that never was on land or sea, the old woman said, "O God, I thank You for these gifts of Your love on this Christmas Day. You have given me all these and Christ." You know as well as I do, if you are only true to your own heart, that you would rather have this old woman's heart's ease than all the wealth in the world. What is it worth to a man, if surrounded with all luxury, and all wealth at his command to minister to every desire of his material body, if his heart is hot and restless, if he vexes himself every day, and is filled with a great hunger that cannot be fed? That was Lot's condition. It was a sad failure, that move of Lot's.

But now, Lot, how about your family? When you turned your back on Abram, when you turned your back on the tent, and went to live in Sodom, what about your children? The story is one that cannot be told. It is too dreadful, too appalling. Let it simply be said that when Lot moved into Sodom, and took his children there, he lost them. Oh, the tender infinite grace of God, as seen in the angel sent to give to Lot the message of coming destruction. Upon hearing it Lot went out to persuade his sons-in-law, *but he appeared to his sons-in-law to be jesting.* They laughed at him, and did not pay heed to him, and so he left the city with his wife, whose heart had become bonded to all the grossness of the city; and he left with his two daughters, who had become utterly corrupted in the city. He lost his children; he lost his loved ones when he took them into the city.

And everyone here that knows what that means knows that when Lot erected his tent toward Sodom, he was making a disastrous mistake. Better to stay in the tent, better to be old-fashioned, better to be considered out-of-date and hold on to the children, than to move into the city to get wealth and satisfy the greed of a covetous nature, if the price to be paid is the price of the ruin of the loved ones.

Yet let me ask him another question. But Lot, what did you do for Sodom? Surely you had a good effect upon the men in Sodom. You must have influenced them. Where are they? You went down to purify Sodom, to lift Sodom up, to lift Sodom toward righteousness and God and truth. You know the awful story. There were not ten righteous men in the city. The man that nearly saved Sodom was not the man who went to live in it, but that man under the oaks. He prayed for Sodom, pleaded with God for Sodom, wrestled with God for Sodom, and he received the divine promise that if ten righteous men should be found therein, the city would be spared; but they could not be found, although Lot had lived there until he became mayor. It was a disastrous failure. He lost not only his peace and his children, but also his influence.

And then the last thing. It is the meanest question, but I choose to put it last, and put it in this way. Lot, how much did you make? You know the answer. You do not want me to tell you. If you want to know how much he made out of it, go someday when you are on the other side of the ocean, to that brackish Dead Sea, whose lifeless waves lap the shore with an unending monotone of death. He lost it all. All he saved out of Sodom was his life, and he had to be persuaded to save that. In the end, angel hands put upon his shoulders hurried him out of the city. He went in rich and came out a pauper.

Now you see what I meant when I said, Here is a disastrous failure, a good man who wanted to be right, who, acting upon a wrong principle, took the wrong pathway, pitched his tent toward Sodom, came into Sodom, became chief magistrate of Sodom, lost his peace, lost his children, lost his influence, lost his very wealth at last; and we see him hurrying away, even as he leaves, so demoralized that he longs still for a city, and he says, "Oh, let me escape to Zoar, it is only a little town." He went to Zoar, and did not tarry there, but found his way to the mountains, the caves of the mountains; and when in those lonely mountain caves he has left behind him all the wealth and finds himself back again in the old place of separation from things that are evil, then it is probable that he begins to find his peace, and will finally regain something of his influence.

Now, surely, I do not need to hold you another moment to say anything about the lessons here. They are so self-evident. I want to press them home in the closing words. The first lesson, then, is that there is no folly quite equal to the folly of self-centered seeking. This is the place to declare it. You will not hear that outside; that message is not preached in the ways of men today. It must be in the sanctuary of God, in the house of prayer, that this truth is repeated. Men are urged outside to take care of number one, to look after themselves. You can often tell what the world is thinking by its proverbs, its maxims, its little speeches. Take care of number one. That is a doctrine of devils.

I heard a man say in one of the suburban trains in London a while ago, traveling to the city, speaking of a man who had fallen out of the line of success, "Well," he said glibly, "it is each for himself, and the devil takes the last"; and that is the gospel men are preaching outside. Look out for yourself, each for yourself. Here in the sanctuary of God, I say that that is not true; that in those cases the devil generally gets the first, and it is the man who is self-seeking, and who makes choices in life simply upon the basis of his own selfishness, who is going to make the most disastrous failure.

And the second lesson I learn from this study of the character of Lot is this: It is utterly useless to try and make compromises between good and evil. Lot pitched near Sodom and did not go into Sodom at first. It was an act of dishonesty and hypocrisy. If your heart is in Sodom, you might just as well go in first as last. I have infinitely more respect for the man who goes clean in than for the man pitching just outside and trying to keep up a sort of religiousness while his heart is set upon evil things. You cannot do it. There is no *via media* here. You must find a simple principle of life and act upon it. You may try to pitch your tent near Sodom to keep up an appearance of loyalty to God, and to get out of Sodom everything material and sordid, but it will not last. The man will soon get into Sodom, but at last he will be driven out, a pauper and a beggar. There is no failure more heartbreaking and disastrous than success which leaves God out of the equation.

Oh, my brothers and sisters, you know it. You tell me today about a man amassing wealth, and you say of that man that he is a far-seeing man. How far does he see? Oh, he sees a long way ahead, and he makes his arrangements, and arranges for combinations of business interests. If you think a man is far-seeing because he just sees around the globe and buys all the ships up, you are as blind as he is. The man who is far-seeing is the man who sees off the earth into heaven. If you are simply setting out in life to amass mere material success, fame created or position gained, then success will be the most dismal and disastrous failure.

The far-seeing man is the man who takes up his pen and writes, *If the earthly tent which is our house is torn down, we have a building from God, a house not made with hands, eternal in the heavens* (2 Corinthians 5:1). That is a far-seeing man, a man who has taken into account the spiritual things in his dealing with the material, the man who has taken into account eternity as he is passing through time, the man who has reckoned with the immortal while tabernacling in mortality; that is the far-seeing man, the man whose choice is based upon the right principle, who talks only of everlasting riches and the spaciousness of eternity. That is the far-seeing man. If a man builds the temple of success, broad and radiant and beautiful; if its foundation is earth and its capstone is no higher than the atmosphere, then he is a disastrous failure. If a man builds his character upon the basis of truth, which will find itself in harmony with God, then that man has made a success, though he never makes a fortune, and never makes a name for himself.

Return in conclusion to this statement. Choice is not wrong; it is man's prerogative to choose; it is a proof of the majesty of his being. What are we to do? Choose based upon a right principle.

In conclusion, go back to Abram, the out-of-date man, the old-fashioned man. When Lot made his choice, did you notice in the thirteenth chapter what happened? When Lot had made his choice, and had gone, God said something to Abram. What did God say to Abram? He said, *"Now lift up your eyes and look from the place where you are." Your eyes,* God says. Notice the force of it. A few moments before, Lot had lifted up his eyes; *Lot chose for himself.* God now says to Abram, *"Now lift up your eyes."* Which way is Abram to look? Look to the north, look to the south, and look to the east, look to the west. But that is every way. Exactly.

But a man cannot look north and south and east and west without looking at what Lot has looked at. Exactly. I think I hear Abram say, "I have lifted up my eyes, and I have seen everything there is to be seen." Now God says, *"All the land which you see, I will give it to you and to your descendants forever."*

But that cannot be right. Lot has that. Man does not possess anything except what God gives him. Did Abram choose? Oh yes, before Lot did. What did he choose? He chose not to choose for himself, but to let God choose for him. That is the true principle of choice. You remember the often-repeated lines of Tennyson. Remember these are not the words of the preacher at his desk, but the words of the poet in his sanctuary, the words of the poet looking deeply into the very heart of things, standing for no particular morality, the exponent of no particular creed, or dogma, or doctrine. What did the great poet write for us? He wrote this:

> Our wills are ours, we know not how,
> Our wills are ours, to make them Thine.

That is the philosophy of life upon which Abram lived. He had a will. What did he do with it? He willed to do the will of God. Abram, you had a choice; what choice did you make? "I chose that He should choose for me my law." With what result? Abram got everything; Lot lost everything. Won't you let me press upon you these two principles of life? Will you choose upon a selfish basis, for your own gratification, which is to compromise between good and evil? Or will you rather exercise your kingliness of will by willing that God's will should be supreme? If you will do this latter one, what then? Then you will prove the truth of Christ's words: *Blessed are the meek* (Matthew 5:5 KJV) – the people that are not self-assertive, the people that do not set up themselves as the standard and criterion of desire – *for they shall inherit the earth*. It has always been so.

Take the Old Testament narrative and go through it. Take the New Testament narrative and go through it. Take human history and pass along it. You will always find this so. The people who let God choose get everything, and the people who choose for themselves lose everything. I can well imagine that there was a day when the men of the world laughed at Noah. I have sometimes tried to imagine what the newspaper articles would have been like if newspapers had existed when Noah went into that ark. There would have appeared in all probability a column headed, "Strange Case of Mental Aberration." "Noah, our highly respected fellow countryman, has at last culminated his folly by going into this peculiar structure that he has been building, and he is locked in; he has given up his land and everything, except his own immediate relatives and a curious but carefully selected assortment of living things."

But there came a day when the only landowner in the world was Noah. There came the morning after the deluge and desolation and despair and darkness when Noah came out and the whole earth belonged to him. That is always so. Are you a little in doubt about it? Do not try and read all your life story in the appearances of these hours. Go back to history, and you find that it is always so. May God help you to choose upon the true principle; and letting Him choose, enthrone Him in your life, make Him absolute Monarch, handing over the reins of government to the King, flinging back the door of every chamber of the being, letting Him master you.

Then will your life be in harmony with His will, the horizon will be set back, and the light breaking upon you will be the light that has no waning, the dawning of the eternal day. May we be delivered from the folly of Lot and be brought into the wisdom of Abram.

G. Campbell Morgan
– A Brief Biography

D r. George Campbell Morgan began preaching at thirteen – an age when most young men are focused on just about anything but ministry – and spent more than sixty years in the ministry before he stepped into glory. After preaching that first sermon at Monmouth Methodist Church, he regularly preached as a "boy preacher" in country chapels on Sundays and holidays.

Morgan was born on a farm in Tetbury, England, on December 9, 1863. His father was a member of the strict Plymouth Brethren but eventually became a Baptist minister. Campbell Morgan received private tutoring at home because of poor health as a child. He was ten years old when the renowned Dwight L.

Moody came to England to preach for the first time, and that visit inspired Morgan to want to be a preacher.

In 1886, at the age of twenty-three, Morgan left the teaching profession and devoted himself to preaching and Bible exposition. He was ordained to Congregational ministry in 1890. At the age of thirty-three and at the invitation of D. L. Moody, Campbell Morgan visited the United States for the first time in 1896. He was a guest lecturer for the students at the Moody Bible Institute. This was the first of fifty-four times he crossed the Atlantic to preach and teach.

In 1897, Morgan accepted a pastorate in London. There, he often traveled as a preacher and was involved in the London Missionary Society. After the death of Moody in 1899, Morgan assumed the position of director of the Northfield Bible Conference in Massachusetts. After five successful years in this capacity, in 1904, he returned to England and became pastor of Westminster Chapel, London, where he served for the next thirteen years – from 1904 to 1917. Thousands of people attended his services and weekly Friday night Bible classes.

From 1911 to 1914, he was also the president of Cheshunt College in Cambridge, which eventually merged with Westminster College. He left London for the United States, where he conducted a fourteen-year itinerant preaching and teaching ministry.

He had no formal training for the ministry, but his devotion to studying the Bible made him one of the leading Bible teachers of his day. In 1902, Chicago Theological Seminary conferred on him an honorary doctor of divinity degree. Although he did not have the privilege of studying in a seminary or a Bible college, he wrote books that are used in seminaries and Bible colleges all over the world.

Morgan taught at Biola University in Los Angeles, California, for a short time (1927-1928), and at Gordon College of Theology and Mission in Boston (1930-1931). He served as a pastor of the

Tabernacle Presbyterian Church in Philadelphia, Pennsylvania (1929-1932). Finally, in 1932, he returned to England, where he became pastor of Westminster Chapel once again, and remained there until his retirement in 1943.

Westminster Chapel flourished with his teaching, fundraising, and social programs. When he preached, so many people gathered that even police involvement was sometimes necessary. He was a prolific author and sought-after preacher. In his sixty years of ministry, he preached an estimated 23,390 times and wrote about eighty published works. This number does not include the ten-volume set of sermons, *The Westminster Pulpit*, or the sermons that were published independently as booklets and pamphlets, or the works published posthumously. He wrote commentaries on the entire Bible and on many devotional topics related to the Christian life and ministry.

Morgan may have been ahead of his time when he said, "The reason why men do not look to the church today is that she has destroyed her own influence by compromise." Among his popular works are titles such as *Discipleship* (1897), *All Things New, A Message to New Converts* (1901), *God's Perfect Will* (1901), *Evangelism* (1904), *The Life of the Christian* (1904), and *The Practice of Prayer* (1906).

His essay entitled "The Purposes of the Incarnation" was included in a famous and historic collection called *The Fundamentals*, a set of ninety essays edited by the famous R. A. Torrey, who himself was successor to D. L. Moody both as an evangelist and a pastor. *The Fundamentals* is widely considered to be the foundation of the modern Fundamentalist movement.

Morgan was a respected husband and father. He was married to Annie, better known as Nancy, and they had four boys and three girls. His four sons followed him into the ministry.

He was instrumental in bringing Martyn Lloyd-Jones to Westminster in 1939 to share the pulpit and become his successor.

Morgan was a friend of F. B. Meyer, Charles Spurgeon, and many other great preachers of his day.

Morgan died on May 16, 1945, at the age of 81.

* * * *

"What we do in the crisis always depends on whether we see the difficulties in the light of God, or God in the shadow of the difficulties."
– G. C. Morgan

Other Similar Titles

Following Christ, by Charles H. Spurgeon

You cannot have Christ if you will not serve Him. If you take Christ, you must take Him in all His qualities. You must not simply take Him as a Friend, but you must also take Him as your Master. If you are to become His disciple, you must also become His servant. God-forbid that anyone fights against that truth. It is certainly one of our greatest delights on earth to serve our Lord, and this is to be our joyful vocation even in heaven itself: *His servants shall serve Him: and they shall see His face* (Revelation 22:3-4).

Charles H. Spurgeon originally wrote this book for members of the Young People's Society of Christian Endeavor. Spurgeon's heartfelt writing style makes this book one that today still encourages believers to move into Christian action. He emphasizes simply moving forward, using the talents and resources you already have at your disposal, for the Lord's service and your own eternal reward. The concepts presented are easy to understand and straight-forward, if only you are ready to lay down your life to follow Christ.

Available where books are sold.

Holiness, by J. C. Ryle

He who wants a correct understanding of holiness must first begin by examining the vast and solemn subject of sin. He must dig down very deep if he wants to build high. Wrong views about holiness are generally traceable to wrong views about human corruption.

Practical holiness and entire self-consecration to God are not given adequate attention by modern Christians. The unsaved sometimes rightly complain that Christians are not as kind and unselfish and good-natured as those who make no profession of faith. Far too many Christians make a verbal proclamation of faith, yet remain unchanged in heart and lifestyle. But Scripture makes it clear that holiness, in its place and proportion, is quite as important as justification. Holiness, without which no one shall see the Lord (Hebrews 12:14). It is imperative that Christians are biblically and truly holy.

Available where books are sold.